GAIL SCOTT

ESSAYS ON HER WORKS

WRITERS SERIES I I

SERIES EDITORS:

ANTONIO D'ALFONSO AND JOSEPH PIVATO

Guernica Editions Inc. acknowledges the support of
The Canada Council for the Arts.
Guernica Editions Inc. acknowledges the support of the
Ontario Arts Council.
Guernica Editions Inc. acknowledges the financial support of
the Government of Canada through the Book Publishing
Industry Development Program (BPIDP).

GAIL SCOTT

ESSAYS ON HER WORKS

EDITED BY LIANNE MOYES

GUERNICA
TORONTO·BUFFALO·CHICAGO·LANCASTER (U.K.)
2002

Lianne Moyes, Guest Editor
Guernica Editions Inc.
P.O. Box 117, Station P, Toronto (ON), Canada M5S 2S6
2250 Military Road, Tonawanda, N.Y. 14150-6000 U.S.A.

Distributors:
University of Toronto Press Distribution
5201 Dufferin Street, Toronto, Ontario, Canada M3H 5T8
Independent Publishers Group
814 N. Franklin Street, Chicago, Il. 60610 U.S.A.
Gazelle, Falcon House, Queen Square, Lancaster LA1 1RN U.K.

Typeset by Selina.
Printed in Canada.
First edition.

Legal Deposit – Fourth Quarter
National Library of Canada
Library of Congress Catalog Card Number: 2002102610
National Library of Canada Cataloguing in Publication Data
Main entry under title:
Gaill Scott : essays on her works
(Writers series ; 11)
ISBN 1-55071-164-4

1. Scott, Gail – Criticism and interpretation. I. Moyes, Lianne.
II. Series: Writers series (Toronto, Ont.) ; 11.
PS8587.C.623Z67 2002 C813'.54 C2002-900482-9
PR9199.3.S35Z67 2002

Contents

Acknowledgments

I would like to thank the journals *Trivia*, *Tessera*, *Studies in Canadian Literature*, *Trois*, *Meta* and *Canadian Review of Comparative Literature* as well as the presses of the University of Toronto and Wesleyan University-University Press of New England for permission to reprint the essays collected here. Individual acknowledgments follow each essay. I am also grateful to the contributors for the combination of patience and energy they devoted to the process of revision. My special thanks to Simon Hopkins for looking after our children while I worked, to Licia Canton, Joseph Pivato and Antonio D'Alfonso for their support, and to Nabeela Sheikh for her editorial assistance. The preparation of this collection was enabled by grants from Fonds pour la formation de Cherchcurs et d'Aide à la Recherche, Québec, and the Social Sciences and Humanities Research Council of Canada. Dialogue with Gail Scott made the work a pleasure.

Introduction

"An Affective In-Between"

LIANNE MOYES

"What exactly is an affective in-between between theory and experimental writing?" asks Camille Norton in "After Reading Gail Scott's *Spaces Like Stairs*." Norton's question, raised in an essay which exceeds the distinction between the literary and the theoretical, confronts us with the work of body, senses, movement and emotion in the processes of reading and writing. The other essays in this collection are not, perhaps, as interested as Norton's in the specific project of foregrounding their writing subject or their continuities with the texts they read. Each essay operates within a particular horizon, often according to protocols which were the condition of its initial publication.[1] Yet each essay, in its way, explores the "affective in-between." To make this assertion is to take Norton's concept slightly out of context but not, I hope, to diminish its capacity to speak to Scott's writing practice. To make such an assertion is also to misrepresent somewhat the focus of individual essays, none of which announces "affect" as its subject. However, this introduction does not pretend to do justice to the readings of each critic; it can only hope to provide a point of entry into those readings, to be a provocation to read.

A shared engagement with the problematics of subjectivity and affect, perception and aesthetics – however differently that engagement manifests itself in each essay – is a symptom of several tendencies in literary studies, among them 1) the renewed interest in the historical avant-garde among experimental writers and critics of their work, 2) the interdisciplinary project of situating a given medium (in this case, writing) in relation to others (music, visual art, film and so forth), and 3) the feminist, lesbian and gay projects of thinking through the body/senses. Throughout the 1990s, questions related to subjectivity and affect, aesthetics and perception, questions which were very present to feminist thinkers, for example, in the 1980s, have gained wider currency in literary studies. Literary criticism, which has worked throughout the twentieth century to banish, disguise or otherwise contain the effects of its concern with subjectivity in order to construct itself as a science, a legitimate discipline, is more able at the turn of the twenty-first century to admit to having some truck with affect.

Insofar as it introduces the subject into the relationship between writing and reading, and makes no attempt to differentiate its own language practice from the language practices it discusses, Norton's essay inhabits the "affective in-between between theory and experimental writing." Although it italicizes

"Ottawa

citations from *Spaces Like Stairs*, the essay does not introduce or comment on these citations in conventional ways. Rather, it intercalates fragments of Norton's and Scott's discourses in ways that suggest their radical continuity with one another. Both *Spaces Like Stairs* and Norton's "After Reading" are "passionate fictions" (de Lauretis 3) which have a way of dreaming each other in unforeseen directions, and both perform the contradictions that constitute subjectivity. Body, sexuality, memory, language, emotion, psyche, sensibility, modes of expression, social location, cultural investments are, for them, sites of questioning, process and internal heterogeneity. In Norton's practice, engaging with the text of another is not a matter of finding an appropriate theory/method of inquiry to interpret a given object of study; it is a matter of opening spaces of (erotic) exchange between women, spaces of overlap and self-division, spaces which unfold "like stairs" to accommodate difference and change. Theory emerges in the movement between texts and in the movement of thinking, sensing bodies across various kinds of borders. "[T]here is always a border," writes Norton in her reflections on the material condition of the lesbian novel, "[t]he border one traffics in order to be intelligible." This border, which Norton finds within feminism, within the French language, within Montréal, within academic discourse, within her poems, within herself, is another way of understanding her sense of an "affective in-between."

The temporality of writing, that is, the extent to

which writing unfolds in time, in a process which diffuses the subject as much as it brings her into focus, is central to Nicole Markotic's reading of *Heroine*. Scott's novel, if it can be said to be "about" anything, is about the contradictions and vicissitudes of this process, a process which allows the heroine to resist the various scripts that threaten to immobilize her. The problem of temporality helps explain Markotic's sense that in *Heroine* "from the very first sentence, the book *is* the middle," that "the entire novel is *in medias res*"; it also explains the tendency she finds in *Heroine* (and which she mimes in her own writing) to return again and again to the beginning, thereby insisting that the beginning is arrived at through writing rather than existing prior to writing. In *Heroine*, the processes of constructing a self and coming to write are tied to one another; both are part of the heroine's process of "translat[ing] her body into its own text." If sensory experience, including the pleasure of masturbating in the tub, allows the heroine to "send" and "suspend" herself, it also provides pivotal images for shifts between time frames, urban spaces and angles of vision. Markotic's essay, insofar as it shows body, senses, memory and so forth to be subject to the drift and deferral of writing, offers an innovative way of thinking Scott's investment in the "affective in-between."

Frank Davey's "Totally Avant-garde Woman: *Heroine*" opens with the question, "[h]ow can a woman be a 'heroine,' socially and/or politically, when she is recurrently haunted by her desire, hunger, self-dissatisfaction, emptiness, lack?" The essay goes on to emphasize both the constructed nature of lack and the strategies Scott's novel uses to undercut the discourses which reinforce the heroine's self-doubt. Shame, a source of ambivalence in the heroine insofar as it is what paralyzes her and what she fights most ardently against, is the principal affect under study in Davey's essay. This is not surprising if we consider Davey's explicit concern with the intersecting discourses of the social, political and personal, with what might be described as "the affective sources and consequences of social injustice and inequalities of power" (Adamson and Clark 2). In *Heroine*, shame stems variously from a sense, albeit tongue-in-cheek, of genital deficiency ("Oh Mama why'd you put this hole in me?"), of anglo guilt, of being unable to fit into one group or another, of having sold out to one group or another, of being inadequately loved, of loving oneself inadequately. There is a certain self-reflexive humour, Davey shows, in the narrative presentation of the heroine's anxiety: "a heroine can be sad, distressed, it just has to be in a social context" (*Heroine* 84; qtd. in Davey).

In Jennifer Henderson's reading of *Main Brides*, subjectivity becomes "an extreme form of receptivity and porosity" and the body "an aesthetic surface" which enables "the material production of identities." Sensory experience of all kinds – not just the volley of *looks* on the street and in the bar, but also the more proximal exchange generated by the bar's music and the presence of bodies – is key to the portraits drawn by Lydia, the narrator/porous interface of Scott's novel. As Henderson points out, the "layered arrangement" and "rhythmic sampling" of music which Lydia takes in while watching Nanette, for example, become a way of capturing the "moving palimpsest" that is Nanette. In *Main Brides*, subjectivity – that of Lydia and her "subjects" – is an aesthetic effect, an effect of feeling "free enough to take in all external impressions" (*Main Brides* 132; qtd. in Henderson). Insofar as it links perception to "self-invention, movement and hope for women in a social context of rampant misogynist violence," Henderson's essay participates in the contemporary project of redefining the aesthetic. As elaborated by Jennifer Fisher, this project involves a dynamic sense of the aesthetic, not just as a particular style or theory of art but "as a *relational form*, one which can account for the connections attendant in processes of identification, social affiliation and discursive practice" and as a form of "*sensory mediation* of social states and cultural formations" (4). In Henderson's essay, the aesthetic is no "apolitical formalism" (Fisher 4); it is a process of "[l]ooking for . . . information on how to make an art out of [life]" (*Main Brides* 55; qtd. in Henderson).

Early in her essay, Carla Harryman reminds us that Gail Scott "originally wanted to call [*Main Brides*] an installation." An installation, here, might be understood as a series of relations between different parts assembled within a given site, a site through which one moves, multiplying the lines of the gaze and making one's own connections among various media. The idea of an installation helps illustrate Harryman's argument that Scott's narrative never pretends to stand outside the particular community – "comprised of gay, lesbian, bisexual, straight people, dark people, immigrant people" – which it narrates. "In *Main Brides*," Harryman observes, "the anticipatory state is also the participatory state." Like an installation, the narrative brings readers, characters, narrators into a performative and affective space, the space of "another approach to History" (*Main Brides* 98; qtd. in Harryman) in which the aesthetic is also, potentially, the real. The relationship between the aesthetic and the real is key to Harryman's sense of the way André Breton's avant-garde work on autobiography haunts Scott's novel. "[C]ontaminate[d]" with the writer's biography as well as with invented characters whom one has a feeling one has seen on The Main, she suggests, *Main Brides* becomes a point of transfer for women in the process of engaging the aesthetic and becoming (real).

Barbara Godard's "Writing from the Border: Gail Scott on 'The Main,'" too, is concerned with "women . . . who will connect art and life to make a new history based not on violence but on aesthetic detail." However, her essay moves the problematics of subjectivity and affect, aesthetics and perception, in another direction, one which situates Scott's writing practice in terms of her cultural location as an anglophone in Quebec: "Writing between languages has obliged her to invent her very medium, to engage in "language-centred" work on signs as affective and effective

relays rather than as cognitive representations and so
to make English vibrate differently with (Latin)
rhythms from Quebec." Drawing on the work of
Deleuze and Guattari, Godard's essay explores the
"minor" practice of English in Scott's texts, particularly their "intensive" or "asignifying" use of language
which emphasizes sound, texture, pattern, performance and address more than meaning. "Language,"
Godard explains, "carries a story of the passions of
the individual body." In Godard's view, pauses, shifts,
parentheses – any form of border play which opens
"a space of the in-between, of the gap or excess of
signification" – allows the "unleashing [of] pathos,
affect." This play along borders, she shows, operates
in many registers simultaneously in *Main Brides*, mo-
bilizing "the logic of outside in/inside out, of the
moebius strip," exposing the paradoxes of Quebec-
Canada relations, reading the traces of waves of
immigration in signs along The Main, fracturing narrative consciousness, allowing one thing to become
another, generating the subject through a series of
relations, re-conceptualizing "writing as research into
the as yet unthought."

Working within the framework of translation
studies and re-conceptualizing the translator as a
co-creator of "hybrid literary texts . . . informed by a
double culture," Sherry Simon's essay reads *My Paris*
as a work of translation. Translation, she argues, is
figured within the novel by the comma which stands
between French and English versions of a word or
expression. In this way, *My Paris* points "towards a

space which holds increasing significance in the contemporary world: the space where multiple languages
gather, where translation and writing express the
same impulse to use language contact creatively." For
Simon, this gathering of languages, this project of
making the text "a crossroads of sensibilities," differs
from the modernist use of translation for "aesthetic
innovation." The comma of translation renders the
French language visible, audible, in the pages of
Scott's English-language text in a way that it never
was, for example, in the pages of Gertrude Stein; the
comma is also, for Simon, a reminder of Walter
Benjamin's sense of translation as a process which
reveals differences rather than one which transmits
messages. Simon's essay, not unlike Godard's, finds
in Scott's writing a preoccupation with "a space in-
between, a space of blurred categories and undecidability," a space which resists "explanation or
interpretation."

   In Dianne Chisholm's essay, the "affective in-between" manifests itself in the figure of the *flâneur*, as
well as in the *flâneur*'s Benjaminian composition
strategies of allegory and montage. Characterized by
Chisholm as a "chronicle of walks," "a series of stops
in a daily passage through the city," "a collection of
objects of perception," *My Paris* juxtaposes a city of
sensory pleasure with a city of suffering, producing a
discontinuous allegory which makes legible the ruins
of capitalism and the legacy of colonialism. The porous subjectivity which confounds relations between
self and other in *Main Brides* is here dispersed "among

objects of spontaneous association." As Chisholm points out, the *flâneur*'s syntax, with its abundance of participles and sentence fragments, allows objects to take form as the *flâneur* perceives them (without giving her precedence over them), and emphasizes the *flâneur*'s movement through the city (without producing the illusion of progress). Ambivalence marks the *flâneur*'s relationship to the aesthetic. Indulging the senses, Chisholm suggests, is part of the pleasure the *flâneur* takes in cruising Paris and, at the same time, is a way of maintaining the level of intoxication, distraction, necessary to question what she finds. As a "*flâneur* of the interior," sensory experience is something in which she might like, but is unable, to take refuge. The aesthetic, Chisholm demonstrates in "The Dialectics of 'Watching'" section of her essay, has the power to recuperate French revolutionary history for the bourgeois dream; but it is also that which allows the *flâneur* of *My Paris* to read and render legible (via allegory and montage) that very process of recuperation.

As Gail Scott's responses to questions about affect in the interview indicate, her project is one of derailing thinking more than one of conveying emotion. Derailing thinking, moving outside the ordinary circuits, she suggests, involves pushing as many buttons as possible simultaneously, awakening in the body "the fear, the anguish, the pleasure, too"; it also involves analysis, intellectual work. Affect is part of that analysis insofar as it is "a screen for all of the social and political and cultural and personal and geographical particles, captured somehow in syntax, which is music," a screen for "all the things that give tone to a moment in time." This music, Scott suggests in her discussion of Lawrence Braithwaite's writing, does not speak to us in conventional terms; it lets us know indirectly, obliquely, "the ef-fects of various kinds of social oppression, marginalization," as well as "highly dignified and imaginative responses to those oppressions." As a screen, as music, affect is dynamic, "always in flux," always in-between. In the essays collected here, affect haunts the border be-tween fiction and theory; the process of writing the subject; the interface between personal and political, action and paralysis; the *"relational form"* of the aesthetic (Fisher 4); the overlap, the disjunction be-tween the fictional and the real; the "uncanny edge of language" (*Spaces Like Stairs* 62; qtd. in Godard); the gathering of languages around the comma of translation; and the dialectics of watching which engage Scott's *flâneur*.

NOTES

1   The essays of Camille Norton, Nicole Markotic and Barbara Godard were published in the small magazines *Trivia*, *Tessera* and *Trois*, respectively. The essays of Sherry Simon and Dianne Chisholm were published in journals of scholarly associations in fields adjacent to Canadian literary studies, in the translators' journal, *Meta*, and in the *Canadian Review of Comparative Literature*. Jennifer Henderson's essay was pub-lished in *Studies in Canadian Literature*. The essays of Frank Davey and Carla Harryman appeared in books with Univer-sity of Toronto Press and Wesleyan University Press-Univer-sity Press of New England. The essays of Dianne Chisholm

and Carla Harryman, works in progress when this book
project was launched, were already promised to their respective publishers *CRCL* and Wesleyan UP-UPNE, a circumstance which produced roughly parallel publication dates.

WORKS CITED

Adamson, Joseph, and Hilary Clark, eds. *Scenes of Shame: Psy-
    choanalysis, Shame, and Writing.* Albany, NY: State University
    of New York P, 1999.

de Lauretis, Teresa. *The Practice of Love: Lesbian Sexuality and
    Perverse Desire.* Bloomington; Indianapolis: Indiana UP,
    1994.

Fisher, Jennifer. "Relational Sense: Towards a Haptic Aesthetics."
    Parachute 87 (July-Sept. 1997): 4-11.

After Reading Gail Scott's
Spaces Like Stairs

CAMILLE NORTON

If we exist anywhere it must be as women of our generation.

France Théoret

Moi et l'Autre

In *Spaces Like Stairs*, Gail Scott's collection of essays on writing as a feminist in post-modern Québec, Scott stands at the intersection between the writer and her culture, a space she continuously transforms by the questions she raises about what it means to write.[1] "These essays," she says in her preface, "... are simply (and not so simply) the story of a writer's journey among the literary, theoretical, political signposts of a certain period (the late 1970s and 1980s) in a certain place (Québec)." Scott inscribes the story of this journey with her experience of a particular city, Montréal, where she, as an English Canadian, is both an insider and an outsider in a largely francophone women's culture. The concept of *space*, as Scott explores it here, includes the experience of "nation" in a country divided into French-and English-speaking provinces – spaces of separateness, of dominant and minority cultures, of exile, of difference. The city becomes the space where women of her generation meet to talk about how they write. The space becomes a new city, a woman's city this time, which women writers infuse with *la modernité*, feminism, and the necessity of continuous translation.[2]

The space from which Scott writes – and *towards* which she writes – resounds with the conversations of her friends. *Moi et l'autre*, Scott's term for defining the self in relation to another, approaches difference as the possibility of a creative interchange, an interchange that progressively shatters the mystique of the writer's radical loneliness. Scott suggests that something other than isolation lies between women who write: the surface of the ordinary, words passed across a café table, the material of culture (*that thin layer*). This "in-between" is the vital ground where meaning occurs between two women who begin to recognize each other. Here, in the air between two women speaking about the poem, the story, and their lives, lies the paradigm of space as Scott develops it. For this space to remain vital, it must remain open to the change each woman, by virtue of her history, brings to it. The space is sacred insofar as it is infinitely capable of renewal. None of the spaces Scott invokes is sacred in the sense that its boundaries are time-honored, its laws immutable: . . . *even a space we have "appropriated" thanks to our feminist consciousness*

– must immediately give way to another. So the spaces unroll around us. Like stairs . . . ("Preface").

What happens in the space where women writers talk to each other? In a café on rue Saint Denis, France Théoret places her manuscript on the table between them. They drink coffee. They talk about Virginia Woolf and Colette. Then they discover that in order to talk about their own writing, they must come to terms with the differences between their political histories – the divide between French-and English-Canadian experience.

perhaps the question is how to keep the new space open where women's culture rests (that thin layer) by what forms might we make it resistant to the 1980s avalanche of co-option yes how to state the facts when we are fiction to be imaginative when our fiction is biography when in order not to sink in sadness our fiction must be theory ("Spaces Like Stairs").

In a café on The Main, Erin Mouré reads Gail Scott Olga Broumas's translation of a poem by Odysseus Elytis. *Words of a Greek male poet translated by a Greek-American lesbian, translated again into sound by the voice of Erin, who grew up in Alberta, reading to me, an English Quebecer . . . ("A Visit to Canada").* Meaning poured into the in-between, sifted, relocated, multiplied.

In nearly every instance, these essays collapse the

distinctions between public and private spaces. They continue dialogues begun in cafés, later elaborated at private gatherings of women writers. *I tried to confront that question as the only woman from a Protestant background at a retreat of Quebecer feminist writers in New Brunswick in August, 1980. To confront "body" – especially as a vehicle of memory. I couldn't have found a more ideal situation to start this reflection ("Red Tin + White Tulle").* They borrow from notebooks that record the process of a novelist grappling with the impossibility of the heroic trajectory for her female "heroine." *I'm getting a clearer picture of her, she's becoming a fictional character who belongs to the streets of the city. I'm the voyeur . . . ("Paragraphs Blowing on a Line").* They remake the city according to terms circulated in cafés and apartments, Montréal as it is seen in winter from a window in a writer's room. *Fittingly, outside it is a grey November day. Through my window on Jeanne Mance St. is a suite of three-dimensional planes. The bare trees in the immediate foreground. Across the street, the rounded garrets, the fancy trim on top of the turn-of-the-century houses ("A Feminist at the Carnival").*

Moi et l'autre: the psychic doubleness of a city long politicized by the visceral politics of language. The bilingualism of a French majority forced to conduct its public life in English. The bilingualism of the dominated, an economic imperative; the bilingualism of the dominant, a facile gesture when it was made at all. All of this began to change in the 1970s, with the victory of the Parti Québécois in 1976, but to be a feminist in Québec in 1989 is to be aware of "versions" of feminism, the result of childhoods accented by differences of class and religion. For Gail Scott, the child of the dominant culture, and for France Théoret, the child of the dominated, there could be no feminist theory that ignored difference for the sake of "the common condition of all women."

Admittedly, clearing that first small hurdle of nation was itself no small matter. Not only was the weight of our respective national histories with us, but also our childhood memories of Eastern Ontario and Québec in the 1950s. In the half-French village where I grew up, the English spoke of "the French" with disparagement, forcing on them a hundred humiliations, including the refusal of French-language high schools. Thus, the French students, unable to cope in English, often ended their schooling with grade nine ("Virginia and Colette: On the Outside Looking In").

In the 1940s, at the Pensionnat des Saints Anges, in Saint Jérome, the Sisters of Saint Anne instructed my mother in French. At fifteen, "unable to cope" in English, she took a job filling prescriptions at Sarrazin et Choquette, the large French pharmacy in Montréal, near the old Depuis et Frères. When I asked her whether she made English friends there, she replied with a razor in her voice, "Me? Never!"

In Philadelphia in 1969, Madame Guerin, an American, pursed her mouth whenever I recited in my deplorable Canadian accent. Patois, not really French at all, my mother's language a kind of comic rendition, jokester French, huckster French, a dialect those people speak in the colonies.

Moi et l'autre.
Voulez-vous me donner un petit bec, Maman?
That thin layer of culture.

What We Claim

The customs official in Montréal asks us whether we are related to each other. You say we are cousins, and I shift nervously, aware of the quarter ounce of pot in my bag, the three hundred dollars worth of books, unclaimed, my urgency to cross the border without incident. I have a mark on the side of my neck from when you kissed me on Saint Denis. Last night, in the rain, after all the bars had closed. We can claim that much, you said. That there's blood between us. Perhaps it's enough. Neither of us looks like an "authentic" American, he assumes our families crossed over sometime in the last half-century, to feed off U.S. industry. Paper mills and steel plants, stucco houses, public schools. He's got an alarming amount of the detail right, and from where he sits he can probably tell that we smell the same. Our English is flawless, neither one of us speaks French well anymore, we forgot it while we were growing up. We have, what's the term, been assimilated. Into his meaning of us. Which takes stock of the fact that we really don't belong anywhere. As women. Though he's missed our purpose, our explanations. That's O.K. too, this is neither the time nor the place. I'm relieved to see that he approves of us enough to stamp a date inside our passport books. If you declare nothing more than what's obvious, you can travel anywhere. You can pretend that you know what you mean when you say you are going home.

And my narrator prefers that the meaning be in another language. For she has consciously chosen her minority situation – which is very different than being colonized, when meaning happens in the other language and it's out of your power to do anything about it ("Paragraphs Blowing on a Line").

This is the material condition of the lesbian novel. The lesbian novel that chooses to irradiate the condition of exile, to reorganize "the real" around the erotic interchange between two women who remain invisible as lovers to the man at the border. And there is always a border. That too is the material condition of the lesbian novel. The border one traffics in order to be intelligible.

ॐ

heory Theory/Fiction

the problem is in the space if the mind works best without these distinctions between reality/theory/fiction then the space has slipped from which the essay can spring you're repeating yourself says the voice ("Spaces Like Stairs").

Reading these essays, I encounter two "bodies" of theory to which I respond with acute pleasure in the first instance and with a certain wariness in the second. The first "body" is the theory that Gail Scott offers us here – a writer's theory emerging from the creative process, a theory whose logic is fundamentally artistic, dynamic, practical. It does not – and cannot – survive outside the creative text, outside the novel, for example, or outside the essay relying upon the devices of fiction either; it exists in integral relation to a kind of writing Gail Scott calls "fiction-theory." Her novel, *Heroine*, in which the narrator scrutinizes her relationship to the protagonist, "embodies" fiction-theory.

When a narrator discards the authority implicit in her position, she places herself in a theoretical relation to "story," to the idea of what a story is. As a result, she actively revises what "story" means, and for women writers this revision of genre is a political act. When the narrator of Christa Wolf's *The Search for Christa T.* interrupts her own narrative in order to question the purity of her agenda ("Why am I using Christa T.?

How can I represent her when I never knew her?"),
the writer is wrenching open an ethical space within
a genre many readers regard as innocent, value-free
art, "only a story." In the fiction-theory she enacts in
Heroine, Scott recognizes the political implications of
plot and goes one step further. She struggles with the
conventions of genre to make (an)other kind of story
– to construct a conceptual frame through which the
heroine becomes intelligible.

*you're repeating yourself says the voice the essay needs
logic to be clear to avoid barbarism certain forms must
be borrowed from the dominating culture at any rate
there's no danger of self-betrayal for you women are
excellent at translation women are skilled at stepping
into spaces (forms) created by the patriarchal superego
and cleverly subverting them ("Spaces Like Stairs").*

The second "body" of theory I encounter in these
essays lies *behind* Scott's writing, in the sense that it
"engenders" and feeds much of the intellectual mus-
cle of her work. This is the theory of the French
theorists – Derrida, Barthes, Lacan, Sollers – called
Deconstruction. As it has been rearticulated – and, in
many cases, radically reworked – by French feminists
like Cixous and Irigaray, Deconstruction has had a
second incarnation, called *l'écriture au féminin*,
known in the U.S. as French feminist theory. And, in
the U.S., both Deconstruction and *l'écriture au
féminin* live, for all ostensible purposes, within the
academy.

Where do I live?
It seems I live in the in-between, the space of crossing over and return.

When I say that this theory "lives" within the academy, I mean this in a practical sense, in a writerly sense. Academics, including many women, "practice" French theory within their own critical writing. In other words, they "apply" French theory to the writing of literary criticism. They apply it like an adhesive to a form that remains impervious to radical change. The academic critic – of whatever theoretical stripe – borrows a position of authority when she stands in relation to a text, not only to the text she analyzes but to the text she makes as the analyst. Her body is lost to the academic performance. Even when she is writing "about" the body as a textual "issue," her body is excluded from the writing, for to borrow a position of authority in patriarchal discourse, to speak from behind the mask, is to leave the body of the speaker behind. When the body is left behind, and when the structure of discourse remains unaltered by one's participation in it, the practice of theory fails as a political action.

"Did she put on his knowledge with his power
Before the indifferent beak could let her drop?"[3]

Who is this "she"?
Where is my body in this text?
In between? Or already crossing over?

(Women are skilled at stepping into spaces.)

What exactly is an affective "in-between" between academic theory and experimental writing? An especially urgent question in relation to women's writing in Quebec, where feminism in the 1970s cut its teeth on language theory – on Derrida, Barthes, Irigaray – at a time when Québec attempted secession from Canada on the grounds that the language differences of French Quebecers had become political differences. For women like Scott who were beginning to write, and who were becoming feminists at this moment of political explosion, the second "body" of theory – the theory I associate with the academy – was never academic. It was political theory in a political context.

I am beginning to see how this question must be addressed differently in the U.S., where the politics of language emerge from a complex experience of emigration, slavery, and "naturalization." The experience, for example, of Black English as it is spoken and written in communities (and in literature), and its uneasy status in urban schools, where educators teach dominant discourse as a survival strategy. (And it is a survival strategy.) The experience of multi-cultural Spanish-speaking populations within the U.S., populations "marked," stressed, accented by the effects of different colonial relationships to the U.S. (Mexico and Puerto Rico, among others). The political battles which are beginning to rage in debates and in legal

decisions about the fate of English as the official
language of the U.S.

*Yet, as I read Cixous and the other new French femi-
nists, I felt a strangeness: a feeling that my relationship
to my body might be different than theirs. I began to
think about how one's body is not only gendered, but
is also linguistic, cultural, economic ("Red Tin +
White Tulle").*

Yes. And yet. What exactly is an affective in-between
between theory and experimental writing?

She Whispers

*Our writing-about-writing is also about women occu-
pying a space usually left to an "interpretive milieu"
of critics and the academy – a milieu of great importance to us, but whose particular agenda isn't always
ours ("Preface").*

I was thinking about a poem I wrote ten years ago. It
was a poem I wrote about the linguistic bond I shared
with my mother, a French-Canadian woman who
spoke to me in a language my American father
couldn't understand. I recalled it in order to rethink
the concept of *l'écriture au féminin*, the theory that
women shift fitfully between two languages while
possessing neither completely: the language of the
dominant discourse belonging to the Father, and the

muted, half-articulated language of the Mother, in-
herent in the body.

It's not the idea of "shifting between" that I mind –
it's the idea of not possessing, of falling into language
only to discover that it isn't part of a female's inheri-
tance. That I am, in relation to discourse, either a
voyeur or a thief. French feminist theory. What my
colleagues in the English department call "sexy theory." At Warren House, in the upper Seminar Room
(until recently the preserve of the Old Guard), the
Feminist Colloquium presents another round of papers on writing the body MLA style. Papers on cross-
dressing, on voyeurism, on thievery, on prostitution.
Prostitution very in this year, among the academics.
Women as prostitutes of the pen, and so on. Sexy
theory. I'm suspicious of it. Every time I look closely,
I catch sight of the rakish bodies of *les frères* Jacques
– Derrida, Lacan. And their father, Freud.

*We women have two ways of speaking. The first begins
in our mother's womb as we listen to the rhythms of
her body (likewise for our brothers). As girls, we
continue to develop this largely oral tongue in our
ongoing relationship and identification with her (here,
says Freud, our brothers start to differ). But at the
same time we are developing another relationship to
the "fathertongue" of education, the media, the law –
all patriarchal institutions. Consequently, we end up
with a split relationship to language: there is the
undernurtured woman's voice, badly heard outside in*

what my mother always called a "man's world," and the other language, the one we try to speak in order to bridge the gap ("Shaping a Vehicle for Her Use").

I was thinking about the poem.
A poem about female conspiracy, beginning with an act of sabotage. (I wrote it slantwise, fast, sensing that memory resists the systematic probe.)

It begins with her whisper. It is, in fact, one long whisper, the sound of the symbolic as it is transferred from the body of the mother to the body of the daughter. We are going to do something to him, and he will never know. While he lies sleeping, we're going to help ourselves. She whispers, "Quick, quick, before your father . . ." I grasp her meaning in an instant, retain it in my cells.
Before my father notices we are gone.

A state of emergency.
This experience of female language.

We are taking his bottles down to the basement. Into the coal and pitch-tar scent. Near the furnace in the glowering dark. Whiskey, whiskey, whiskey. Swirled into the drain. His power, we think we've identified it, we think we can rid him of it. She's thirty-two years old, I'm four, we whisper, we empty all the bottles inside the tub in the basement laundry. We empty the three-day drunk. We empty the source of his rage. We empty all the bottles. It's mythic. Because I say so.

It's winter. Because of the coal fire. She told me to hurry. She told me I shouldn't tell. I was her girl. I would never tell.

Duplicity and silence.
This experience of female language.

I thought he was outside our speech, outside our plot. That I had exiled him, floated him in otherness – out there. I thought I was writing my story. Her story. Ours. The mother as anarchist, the daughter as apprentice, female language in the basement of the house like a bomb.

The contradiction is that in delving into memory by letting language take us where it will, we tend to uncover things we intended to repress ("Red Tin + White Tulle").

Now, reading this poem, the poem from which I'd excised him, I experience the shock of "reading" him everywhere. Fear of him sticks to every word, it sticks to the pattern of the words, the hissed, slurred whisper she taught me. When I grasped her meaning. Instantly. Retaining it in my cells. She taught me that, but not in words. Through smell. The pressure of her hand. Her eyes signaling what she couldn't speak. Wouldn't speak? And then, outside of lyric time, he woke up. What happened when he woke up? I can't remember. I never wrote a poem about what happened when he woke up.

Memory, then, as a reconnaissance operation. A tool for writing, but not as mere description. "Je n'écris pas la mémoire, je la travaille," says a Québec friend ("Red Tin + White Tulle").

What Is / What Happens

What exactly is an affective "in-between" between theory and experimental writing? Not one question. A series of questions. What is the life-span of writing that depends on theory-texts for its terms? How do we keep the space from becoming the closed circle, the specialized semantic field of those conversant with but alienated from academia? Questions that come close to the bone.

Questions that can be answered only in the writing. I think of a comment made by the American poet, Denise Levertov: *To the pure, all things are pure, to the poet all things give forth poems.* It is true that I test the "charge" of literature as a writer first and foremost. Then, later, I remember my place in history, in ideology, and the process of referentiality begins. So too with feminism. It existed first as an experience, as an outraged body-consciousness, cellular, intuitive. Then, as a theory that brought me into contact with a community of women who called themselves feminists. And that, of course, is the rub – that our theories help create our worlds, and help sustain them. To excise the theoretical out of some reactionary notion of poetic or spiritual purity is to guarantee the death of a city. Finally, it's a question of balance. And it's personal.

What happens in the space where women writers talk to one another?

A sound unlike any other. Women talking in the *polis*. The first circle. Electrified by conversation. By *le rapport d'adresse ("A Visit to Canada")*, the attention of one's own generation, of one's own kind. The city as it is redefined by a first circle of friends: women who write talking about how they write, importing and rearranging theory, testing it against writing as it is made, against the essay that is the poem that is theory that is story. *Yes how to state the facts when we are fiction.*

As a woman of my generation, I have had to learn the lesson of coming apart from the idea of a homogenous feminist community. Among friends, I have learned who I am in relation to the differences among us.

Something happens when one speaks to one's own kind. After awhile, one begins to sense one's meaning along the ground, one begins to carry that meaning outside the first circle to the second circle, to the third. This is what Gail Scott has done in this brilliant collection of essays. "For a writer may do as she pleases with her epoch," she writes. "Except ignore it."

NOTES

1   This text first appeared in *Trivia: A Journal of Ideas* 15 (Fall 1989): 70-80.

2   *La modernité* is the term used in Québec for post-structuralist theory that uses language as the entrance into discussions of culture. Scott uses this term where an American would use "Deconstruction" or "French feminist theory"; it suggests to me that post-structuralism in Canada has crossed over into artistic, intellectual and political communities in a way that has yet to occur in the U.S. Scott writes, "[t]his emphasis on language in writing (called *la modernité* in Québec) and its rapport with feminist struggle was at the core of the nurturing literary relationship between France Théoret and me."

3   William Butler Yeats, "Leda and the Swan."

Freedom's Just Another Word / for Nothin' Left to Close

Desire Constructing Desire Constructing in Gail Scott's Heroine

NICOLE MARKOTIC

There's a limit to female desire.[1] This is a story repeated so often we sometimes forget not to believe it. Think of those Classical offerings of the fleeing maiden and the pursuant young man. That female desire might stretch beyond the traditional possibility of being "caught" (in either death or marriage) is still a radical alternative in literature.

Gail Scott's *Heroine*, although it covers the ground and the battle of love, ironically twists the readerly expectation for happily-ever-after. "Story," concerning women, is too often confused with a moralizing content and, according to Rachel DuPlessis, "has typically meant plots of seduction, courtship, the energies of quest deflected into sexual downfall, the choice of a marriage partner, the melodramas of beginning, middle, and end, the trajectories of sexual arousal and release" (151). The entire plot of *Heroine* is the heroine taking a bath and masturbating. Her "quest" is to do it until she can translate her body into its own text. "If 'happily ever after' means anything, it means that pleasurable illusion of stasis" (DuPlessis 178). The narrator, at the same time that she indulges her heroine in the illusion of stasis, propels that character forward in the text, forward to the list of possibilities that makes up the last page.

The text's "heroine" acknowledges the role of past heroines, yet doesn't submit to the tradition of either victim or bride-to-be. Scott develops her novel against that oh-so-central ideal of goal or end-climax within the Bildungsroman structure of self-betterment. The heroine, splashing and pleasuring in her tub, does not aim for the "final goal" of writing a novel. She is, albeit in water rather than ink, writing her *self*. This novel, rather than developing character through plot and closure, instead establishes a character-in-process.

The necessity for such self-construction is glaringly apparent with the staccato "Sir" (9) of the text's first word (after the section title). This word signifies the power of patriarchy, and the inherited imbalance of who addresses whom. Immediately, Scott undercuts the minor city official who speaks that single utterance by pointing out the halting English he uses to politely address a tourist who attempts unsuccessfully to view the city through a pay telescope. The "Black tourist" (9), who does not respond verbally, suggests to Scott's heroine someone else's inarticulated subject-position. Nearly every section in the book begins with a sentence or paragraph about this tourist (who eventually is allowed to lose the adjective), or with remarks concerning a "grey woman," a silent outcast of the Montréal streets. Observed through the telescope, this grey woman is a complex character too minor to be heroine and too recurring to be ignored. The device of "the lens shift" (95) allows the narrative to spiral around, questing its own (pleasure) centre and questioning the location of the subject. The shifting lens presents the main character as not merely soaking her limbs, but also keenly aware of the demanding city that beckons from just beyond her bathroom walls. Just as her body has become the story, submersed in water, so too do the under-observed populate this narrative of self.

Encased in the enamel tub, the heroine constructs the city outside her window not just from the narrator's limited view of it, but with the voice inside the radio that gives broadcasts about the FLQ kidnapping of "ten years ago this month" (13). The "tourist" roams past the hookers, across conversations in the cafés, down rue Ste-Catherine, beyond the line of the narrator's vision. The heroine's desire to write this novel splashes out of the tub long before she does. Her words precede her: "The city. Hot autumn. In an apartment a couple are sitting at a table discussing revolution" (49). The couple she envisions is a perfect couple, their lives together pre-scripted.

The structure of this "novel" opens up possibilities of duality: heroine writing heroine, the heterosexual and the homosexual, memory and rebirth. Yet at the same time it offers more than either/or binaries. The narrator constructs herself from various layers:

she refuses to settle for a single expression of her sexuality, she employs her memory for the purpose of rebirth, she writes that rebirth on top of memory. Divided into three parts, *Heroine* presents itself as a novel at the same time that it challenges what, exactly, a book of narrative fiction might be. Scott divides the text into "I. BEGINNING," (7-70), "II." (71-80), and "III. ENDING" (81-183). The "MIDDLE" virtually disappears because, from the very first sentence, the book *is* the middle. Scott plays with the notion that a story must have a beginning, middle, and end, just not necessarily in that order. As the text's heroine lies in her bath, coming into existence, the story swirls around time and Montréal. This narrative spiral allows particular scenes to accumulate, rather than point directly.

Heroine's heroine begins her quest in the bathroom, the most personal of rooms. And then she leaves the door open. She rises out of her bathtub to stroll into the Montréal morning only after she has composed a character-in-process script for the heroine of *her* novel. This process develops from the narrator's memories of a painful love affair, the collage of noise and sights outside her window, the visit from her friend Marie, and the narrator's own sexual gratification. Lounging in the bathtub, site of luxury and routine, she tells herself stories. Again and again and again. This narrator doesn't desire completion; she doesn't desire ending. She desires desire, and its lack of imposed borders. The novel opens not *in medias res*, because in a sense the entire novel is *in medias res*, but post-coitus in that the narrator is already sunk into the "enamel embrace" (9) of the bathtub, already masturbating, continuing a series of orgasms whose origins trace back to before the first page. And the dénouement changes into a second ending; a second coming.

The narrator achieves successive climax by giving her words away. She divulges them to Sepia: her diary, self, lover, bathtub, heroine, past lover, and ideal text. Sepia delineates *Heroine*'s present, ongoing text. The narrator holds these words out to Marie, as replacement for more bodily offerings. She distorts them into surrealistic poems. She writes them down. She speaks them out loud to herself as well as to the reader: "I'm telling stories" (10). That heroine consigned by tradition to the role of either victim or bride, must be unwritten as part of the process of writing again. Meaghan Morris suggests that the "speaking body of feminine writing is perhaps (like the silent muse) only the condition of possibility for the birth of something other" (66). The narrator, washing herself in her bathtub, uncovers layers of herself that have been written over, identities she must *un*cover in order to *dis*cover. She is not so much ridding herself of dirt and waste; she is making the discarded into fiction, transforming debris into writing. Her determined ablutions ritualistically wash away the romantic and restricting definitions of "heroine" that she has had to confront in her attempts at another model. By the end of the novel, the narrator has given birth to herself, birth to the words that project her onto the page and out into the world beyond her bathroom.

The distance between the words in her head and the words on the page is a measure of the space the heroine creates – "I'm lying with my legs up" (9) – so that she can step out and look back at the opening. "I can't just sit down and write a novel about X," says Scott about her narrative technique. Instead, she develops the writing as "it all happens in the process of writing" (*Spaces Like Stairs* 81). So her novel becomes less about "X," the heroine, than it does about the process of writing that heroine, the process of writing that creates writing.

"If I were to start a novel what would be the opening? Quick, free associate. A shrimp in the labia" (78). That image is not so far removed from the opening of the novel. A woman with her legs up, pleasuring herself with tap water: "Oh froth, your warm faucet's spurting warmly over my uh small point" (36). Once in that position, she is able to tweak the "shrimp" in her labia so that it shifts from a less-than-adequate male sexual organ to a lengthy female one. Who needs a penis when gushing frothy water will better serve? The narrator also refers to her clit as "my widow's beak" (126) or "my dolorous reptile" (60) in coy imitation of the refusal to face directly or speak out loud a woman's sexual organs. Yet, these inappropriate and unusual euphemisms point ironically to their literal counterparts, and to the difficulty a contemporary heroine faces when struggling to name or write her self.

The narrator feels scripted and conscripted into writing an account that others will value as legitimate. At the beginning of the novel, she recalls overhearing a voice that declares, "she should adopt a more self-critical voice" (10). Scott grapples with the old idea that women are "too" subjective at the same time as she transforms an object-character into a subject-character. Shortly after, two lesbians singing their love in a telephone booth instruct the narrator how to write her heroine (who is – and isn't – a heterosexual victim): "We hope the heroine of that story isn't a heterosexual victim. Il y en a trop dans le monde" (31). And Marie, who believes a feminist's responsibility is writing, demands, "How can a woman be centred if she isn't in charge of her words?" (59). Constantly defined as one stereotype or another (an anglo to the surrealist poets, merely female to the revolutionaries, too het for the lesbians), the narrator desires to achieve a less external construction of herself. She begins by writing multiplicity: a minor francophone authority figure on Mount Royal; a "Black tourist" who walks the city on foot and through a telescope; a grey woman who "sits silently" (100) on cold park benches, on cement steps in front of busy cafés or rundown motels; a woman lying in the bathtub.

In the section "(I was a Poet before I was You)," the parentheses indicate the narrator's sense of self previously subverted by her desire to please (to the extent that she wishes to become) her lover. Upon first meeting Jon, for example, the heroine remembers that he was "smiling at me through [his] round glasses" (9). His gaze and appraisal of her she equates with a reflection of herself that coincides in his glasses. And the aesthetics of how the two of them appear together – "we were a beautiful couple, everyone said so" (18) – grows out of her desire to fit or match his ideal of the perfect revolutionary woman who looks the part. In "(I was a Poet before I was You)," the heroine has only half-completed her articulation of her written/writing self. This section marks the importance of the narrator's ongoing struggle to construct herself as heroine for the novel she attempts, in the bathtub, to script. Lying in still water, she not only recalls a former lover, she recalls a former self that exists under the layers of her obsession with Jon. Dreaming herself up as heroine, the narrator slips through the cracks of plot to reclaim her sense of language as poetry, to give herself permission to follow wherever the poetics of narration meander.

The narrator, instantaneously creating the text inside her head, writes the lover *out* of existence as she writes herself *in*. For Scott, who does not wish to end, merely, on a note of revenge (who does not wish to end at all), the revelation is in the writing itself. Scott rejects the final climactic movement, opting instead for the open-ended process of writing the feminine sexual self.

"Now I'm out," the narrator declares, immediately after admitting, "No, that isn't right either" (171). Transforming memory into an exact signifier of events is not the narrator's primary concern. Lying in the tub all day long – maintaining Gertrude Stein's continuous present – she begins to face the possibility of future. The narrator of *Heroine* is discovering how to perform Hélène Cixous's miracle of "writ[ing] her self" (Cixous 875) as active subject into her own text. "I don't want a penis to decorate my body with. But I do desire the other for the other, whole and entire, male or female" (891). The script for *Heroine*, then, will be written out of female desire. The heroine emerges victorious not because she has discovered and subsequently written an accurate account of her own experience, but because she engages in a process of recognizing and expressing her desires: "Oh dream only a woman's mouth could do it as well as you" (9). She actively positions the tub and water as "lover," using the "white froth it's coming coming – please stay warm as a sperm river" (126) to replace not only the lover, Jon, who has denied himself to her, but also Marie, whom she denies to herself. In other words, she is not merely masturbating; she constructs the faucet as an active participant, her outwardly moving desire, rather than let these versions of "lover" construct her as passive recipient.

Scott writes her character by writing that character's desire. And she writes desire by constructing a space within which that character can *safely* desire. The feminine aesthetic, then, demands that the sensual and the erotic metamorphose the noun "woman" into a grammar which is more than noun, a grammar that doesn't yet exist. Her sexual identity, except as scripted within the traditional heterosexual couple, has not yet been written enough for her to step into the role casually. Only as she begins to tell herself her own story does she recognize this absence: "Oh Mama why'd you put this hole in me?" (31). Later, she repeats this same phrase without the question mark. Her hole, her hungry mouth, her ever-tensing cunt is her constructed aesthetic, her poetic process, the expectation of longing against which she begins to write.

Lorna Irvine says of the heroine's self-construction that "the narrator tries stepping through Alice's looking glass in order to discover a new angle" (Irvine 118). She reaches in and reverses the mirror. This process does not dismiss the traditional role of woman-as-object-of-desire, but rather establishes the stronger role of object-desiring, so that the heroine can invent herself as subject-in-process, an invention that subverts the notion that female desire must declare its limits. Through this technique of "tactical reversal and resistance, women are turning their sex-saturation back on the sexuality apparatus (sex you have said we are, sex we will be . . .) and in doing so, women begin to outflank it" (Morris 67-8). And there she is, our heroine, in the bathroom, flanked by mirrors, opening her pores to the experience of nakedness revealed, retraced, and flamboyant.

Once she has written herself out of the bathtub and onto the page, the narrator gives her heroine permission to do the same. And the book, then, comes to its "natural" conclusion. Scott's decision to push

continues to 'write' " (60). *Heroine* opens with imperatives and orders and closes with options and blank pages waiting to be filled. The novel's strategies of closure offer the reader invitations to further openings.

The narrator envisions herself walking calmly and confidently toward her destination. The desire she expresses is not just sexual, but a desire to speak about writing in a way that engages further desire. A desire for the "edge" of freedom. A desire for visual aesthetics. A desire for desire. Because it is not *what* the heroine desires, but *that* she desires. No limit in sight.

NOTES

1   This is a substantially revised version of a text which first appeared in *Tessera* 16 (Summer 1994): 84-96.

WORKS CITED

Blumberg, Marcia. "Rereading Gail Scott's *Heroine*: A Triple Lens of Sighting/Citing/Siting." *Open Letter* 8.2 (Winter 1992): 57-69.

Cixous, Hélène. "The Laugh of the Medusa." *Signs: Journal of Women in Culture and Society* 1 (1976): 875-893.

DuPlessis, Rachel Blau. *Writing Beyond the Ending: Narrative Strategies of Twentieth-Century Women Writers*. Bloomington: Indiana UP, 1985.

Irvine, Lorna. "Words on the Prowl: Quebec Literature and Gail Scott's *Heroine*." *Quebec Studies* 9 (1989-90): 111-120.

Morris, Meaghan. *The Pirate's Fiancée: Feminism, Reading, Postmodernism*. London: Verso, 1988.

Scott, Gail. *Heroine*. Toronto: Coach House, 1987.

——. *Spaces Like Stairs*. Toronto: Women's Press, 1989.

Totally Avant-Garde Woman: *Heroine*

FRANK DAVEY

Oh Mama why'd you put this hole in me?

Heroine 31

How can a woman be a "heroine," socially and/or politically, when she is recurrently haunted by her own desire, hunger, self-dissatisfaction, emptiness, lack?[1] Or when her own society, her own "Mama," has constructed her to herself as hollow, as lacking? The lament to "Mama" which itself haunts Gail Scott's *Heroine* insists on politics rather than biology or essence; the "hole" is not natural to the woman, but has been "put" in her. It puns on the vagina as a "negative" signifier, a signifier through absence, and plays with various psychoanalytic reflections on the construction of female sexuality from Freud's "castration complex" to Irigaray's *This Sex Which Is Not One*. It plays also on a number of Lacan's theorizations – most notably that to become a separate human subject requires the losing of direct knowledge of the world and its replacement by language and its forever inadequate signifiers, and that the regulator of language and its meanings is the Phallus, which thus stands as a sign of its own inadequacy – a reminder of both the loss of metaphysical "truth" and the mere systematicity of the symbolic code of language which has replaced it. Addressed to "Mama," who as a separate subject was herself complicit in the symbolic order of language which enabled her to be so consti-tuted (the capital "M" reminds that "Mama" is a word, a linguistic category), the question not only asks "why did you let me be so constructed as fe-male?" but also "why did you let me be human?" – why did you let me come to exist in language, hungering and desiring, split from certainty and wholeness, compelled to experience a linguistically-mediated world as un-fulfilling and unsatisfying?

The site in which "G.S.," the protagonist of *Hero-ine*, asks her anguished questions and seeks the al-ways-inadequate phalluses – a man's love, a career as a writer – that might fill her "hole" is Quebec, itself the site of both Canada's major "split" from whole-ness and French North America's split from its origi-nating culture. Signs of both these splits also abound in the novel. Quebec nationalist graffiti – "QUÉBEC LIBRE" (45), "QUÉBÉCOISES DEBOUTTE" (28), "SOS FLQ" (144) – glow on its walls. Its francophone characters repeatedly classify themselves and anglo-phone Canadians as "français" or "anglais" as if to reconstitute unity with the two founding nations. The RCMP spies on nationalist, socialist and Marxist organizations alike as if any dissent could endanger a confederal imagination of unity. The "hole" in the central character is thus also a national "hole" – a "hole" in a Quebec that can never be the French utopia which it can imagine, a "hole" in a Canada in which a francophone can never trust "une anglaise," or in which to gain that trust the *anglaise* must "stand up . . . and shout 'Vive le Québec libre' " (90).

*

The aspect which most distinguishes *Heroine* from a feminist novel such as Daphne Marlatt's *Ana Historic* or a "Montreal" novel such as Mordecai Richler's *Joshua Then and Now* is the rigorous way in which it insists that all personal and political identities are constructed in language. There is no Ur-woman to recover, goddess to re-awaken, lost matriarchy to reconstitute, or spurned universals to re-acknowledge. Throughout the novel, various ideologies call out their constituting phrases to the narrator "G.S.," offering her instructions and injunctions: "the relaxed woman gets the man," "qui perd, gagne" (11), "good wool lasts forever" (18), "hysteria is not suitable in a revolutionary woman" (19), "possessiveness reifies desire" (21), "Under capitalism, you get it while you can" (26), "a woman who loves herself doesn't put up with a man who deprives her of affection" (27), "put the best foot forward" (39), "androgyny is beautiful" (54), "You have to live and let live" (54), "a good political movie should bring out the fight in people" (67). Popular songs offer melancholy nostalgia ("I miss you most of all, / when autumn leaves start to fall" [56], "Nobody cares for me" [126]), or romantic defiance ("Je ne regrette rien," sings Edith Piaf [39], "there's no tomorrow, baby" [12], "freedom's just another word for nothing left to lose" [65], sings Janis Joplin). Banners, graffiti, T-shirts, advertisements, photos, TV images and radio voices all add in various languages their own messages. Lacking any possibility of a "real" self, G.S. wanders among their discourses and ideologies, attracted to many of them, trying to be "québécoise" when she arrives in Montreal, to be a Marxist revolutionary when she falls in love with the leader of a Marxist cell, and to be a feminist activist when this relationship collapses. Finally she begins to try to write a novel in which she can re-invent herself as a "heroine" – ". . . could the heroine, in the whole picture, lean even more to darkness than to light?" (160); "[t]he heroine, to balance her particular brand of pain, must constantly strive to find other forms in life and art to express the diffuse and varied tone of poetry in her" (162). That is, G.S. begins to try to construct herself in discourse. By the end of the novel, the "heroine" who began as only a remote and idealized possibility to G.S., distinct from her, begins to become the person she, G.S., I, Gail, friend of Marie, can identify herself as:

> The heroine keeps walking. Wondering why a woman can't get what she wants without going into business on every front. Social, political, economic, domestic. Each requiring a different way of walking, a different way of talking. She looks instinctively for her own reflection in a store window. But it's as yet too dark to see clearly. What if Marie is in Bagels'? (181)

*

In the overall discourse of the Canadian nation, G.S.'s
biography has unmistakable meaning. She is a working-class Ontario girl who grows up beside the Trans-
Canada highway in the ironically named Sudbury
suburb of Lively. Her father is a Sudbury miner who
became mine foreman. Lively is a town where cows
moo "lazily in the cool grass" and where the accepted
view of young women as rural Eves, quick to bloom
and fade, is indicated by the general store calendar of
"a cute little red-cheeked girl biting on an apple" and
by the advice the calendar's "old maid" owner gives
to G.S. – "Watch out, iris stems fade quickly, when
uprooted" (43) – when providing the address of her
Westmount niece. G.S.'s choice of Montreal as the
city to which she will flee from Lively constructs it,
as so often in the English-Canadian imagination, as a
place of glamour, romance, sophistication and art:

> There's something alive about an island city built
> around a mountain that seems so different, alive, ro-
> mantic. It has to do . . . with the boats in the harbour,
> the street fairs on boul. St-Laurent, the sound of
> hooves on cobblestone in Vieux Montreal . . . The
> wandering poets, the sidewalk artists, the ritual bus
> and metro strikes. Baseball and hot dogs; hockey and
> beer. The friendly bars, the snobby bars, the bars that
> are always changing names and faces in an endless
> search for the truly hip. And the food: health food,
> ethnic food, fast food, specialty food, fattening food,

diet food, take-out food, deli food, coffee and crois-
sants and crepes. Food and ambiance, food and dancing, food and drink, drink, and some of the best
cuisine this side of paradise. (McCrea 13)

G.S. arrives at the niece's house at the moment in
1969 that the FLQ blows up the Westmount Ar-
moury. The next day she walks east along downtown
Sherbrooke Street:

Fancy rugs, glasses, lingerie in pink and black and purple. There's nothing like a woman with lace next to
her skin. Very classy, very French. I passed the Ritz.
The suitcase was growing heavy. Suddenly the buildings were lower, sagging even, so they seemed to lean
together. On a wall in fresh white paint was written
QUÉBEC LIBRE. AMOUR ET ANARCHIE . . . I
opened the next door. Its sign said La Hutte Suisse. In
the semi-darkness waitresses carried huge trays of
drafts with their solid arms. The guys in the booths
were skinny with tinted glasses. Little beards on pale
skin. I could see the titles of reading material spread
on the tables, *Le Monde*, *Socialisme québécois*, *Liberté*.
I could tell this was a hangout for radical French intellectuals. It felt so good. I sat as near them as I could,
trying to make eye contact. (45)

When G.S. re-writes this arrival story for her "heroine," she excludes the initial visit to Westmount, and
gives even greater emphasis to the signs of culture and
romance and to the indications that here female
possibilities include not merely "cute little girl" and
"old maid" but also "beautiful woman":

[S]he climbed off the bus from Sudbury. The smoke
hung stiff in the cold sky. At Place Ville-Marie she
found the French women so beautiful with their fur
coats and fur hats under which peep their powdered
noses. If anybody asked, she'd say she wanted a job,
love, money. The necessary *accoutrements* to be an
artist. She immediately rented a bed-sitter. Stepping
off the Metro that night and turning a corner, she saw
the letters FLQ screaming on an old stone wall. Drip-
ping in fresh white paint. Climbing the stairs to her
room she knew she'd come to the right place. (22)

What is fascinating about the signs of art and culture
which *Heroine* attaches to Montreal is the extent to
which these are European as well as Québécois. The
bar G.S. first visits is La Hutte *Suisse*. On its tables are
not only *Liberté* and *Socialisme québécois* but the
Parisian *Le Monde*. Her first Montreal lover is a man
who has raced Formula 1 cars. Her second is Jon, a
young Pole and Marxist leader. She first meets him
in the *Cracow* Cafe amid numerous signs of Europe
and European political theory:

You were sitting under a Polish poster drinking coffee
from a thick cup. Lennon glasses on your pretty nose
. . . some hookers came in. They had snowflakes on
their hair and eyebrows. To keep warm one of them
was dancing wildly. Left foot over right. Until she saw
you had your eye on me. She stopped and stared an-
grily from under her wide pale brow. Very French.
And I noticed she had middle-class skin. Therefore no
hooker, just one of your socialist-revolutionary comrades dressed up to help organize the oppressed and
exploited women of The Main. (23)

G.S.'s relationship with Jon takes her very soon on a vacation to Morocco, and to Hamburg, Gdansk, and Marienbad. "Walking white streets eating almond-cream buns. The falling snow giving an air of harmony" (18). The harmony here is the harmony of the cosmopolitan, which for G.S. is what Montreal signifies – not Quebec culture but Marienbad.

Although G.S. and Jon also travel with their cell, the "F-group," by train to Vancouver, and although hints of other parts of Canada occasionally enter the text, Montreal remains the only Canadian gateway to the exotic, and itself remains predominantly French/European. And despite G.S.'s unhappiness with her relationship with Jon, her feeling of being less beautiful than Quebec women because *une anglaise*, and her gradual disillusionment with the politics of the F-group, Montreal continues in the novel to be exotic and idealized. In a sense it is the lover G.S. has left Ontario for – much like Quebec itself is cast as male English-Canada's love-object in George Bowering's *Caprice*.

*

Recalling the thing She loved, a wedding, and the thing She hated, marriage.

Heroine 47

As well as mapping Canada as a stolid anglophone nation that contains a vibrant, exotic and European-ized Quebec, *Heroine* also maps it as severely fractured by various conflicts concerning gender, wealth, language and sexuality. Here, rather than being "different" from English-Canada, Quebec serves as a metonym for it. In fact, running against both the novel's idealization of Quebec and the Quebec nationalist ideologies proclaimed by many of its revolutionaries is the narrator's involvement with causes that cut across nationalism: particularly causes of economic justice and sexual equality. Although the F-group's individual members are mostly sympathetic to the ideal of an independent Quebec, the F-group's work is, in theory, directed to ending the exploitation of female prostitutes, to unionizing waitresses, and to fighting the Pinochet dictatorship of Chile and, in practice, seems to focus on the sexual conquests and intrigues hinted at by its name. G.S. indeed experiences herself as marked as "different" in the F-group – but less by her cultural and linguistic background than by her gender. Francophone nationalism is virtually taken for granted by her and by most of the novel's other characters; at no point do they subject it to critical interrogation. When the Parti Québécois win the 1976 election, "everybody's happy, although, of course, we'd spoiled our ballots. For revolutionaries cannot support bourgeois-nationalism in any form" (89). But they devote endless intellectual debate to formulating social and political principles about human relations in general, and sexual relations specifically. As a result, *Heroine*'s extensive portrayal of the 1970s cultural ferment in Quebec characterizes that ferment not as peculiarly Quebecois but rather as North American and international. Its intuitions and banners may be nationalist but its social preoccupations are transnational.

The faint but implicit criticism in *Heroine* of Quebec nationalism as poorly considered, and potentially in conflict with the transnational ideals of many of those that espouse it, is echoed in G.S.'s own attraction to Quebec and its national romance. The Quebec she is drawn toward is one marked in her mind not specifically as "French" or "Québécois" but as a place that offers "experience," creativity and love. On her second day she looks "for a cafe where [she] could sit and write" (45). She takes an undemonstrative Quebecois lover for "the experience": "I didn't have much choice if I wanted the experience. Because in that particular period québécoise was beautiful, leaving a low premium on English women" (46). After two years she becomes involved with the F-group because she experiences an immediate sexual attraction to its leader: "You had the sweetest smile I'd ever seen on a man. My first thought was that this was exactly what I wanted" (23). She self-consciously endorses the group's reflexive declarations of support for Quebec independence more to retain her social status in the group and Jon's affection than to express political belief. "Slightly embarrassed, I stand up, raising my glass, and shout 'Vive le Québec libre'" (90). As her unhappiness with her relationship with Jon grows, her fascination with Quebec nationalist politics increasingly yields to interest in individual women and feminist issues. Although one of these women is the ex-revolutionary, lesbian, and now independent film-maker Marie, who continues, she says, to be "profondément indépendantiste" (89), another is the Manchester-born Anne, in whose shelter for battered women (itself a transnational sign) the narrator does volunteer work. Much as she experienced Jon and the F-group as a field of ideological conflict, here too she experiences these women as discursive possibilities, as conflicting pressures upon her from outside. By the end of the novel when she is struggling at last to become her own "heroine," she walks a Montreal street everywhere assailed by assertions of what "must be," what is "trendy," or what one "should" do.

> Eating, she thinks that in the 1980s a story must be all smooth and shiny . . . But walking back down The Main . . . she thinks: Yet I feel this terrible violence in me. In any story, it will break the smoothness of the surface . . . She thinks: Maybe I should talk to someone. Startled by a sudden glimpse of her reflection in a window, she thinks: Maybe I should get a job. Then I could buy one of those second-hand men's coats trendy women wear this year . . . Or else one of those beautiful expresso [sic] pots I saw in the window up the street. (182-183)

By this point in the novel both the glamour of Montreal and Quebec nationalism have implicitly become merely two of numerous discursive claims, two of many "trendy" demands like literary style or "beautiful" espresso pots.

*

> From the mountaintop, the Black tourist turns his tele-
> scope. The grey woman sloshes through a yellow pud-
> dle and climbs some outside stairs. Her sister died
> there. Twas the novocaine before Christmas. She was
> allergic but failed to tell the welfare dentist. (38-39)

From the opening paragraph, *Heroine* is framed by
two figures, ostensibly created by the narrating G.S.
– a male black American tourist who inspects the city
by telescope from the top of Mount Royal and a
"grey" indigent woman who wanders the streets be-
low oblivious to the telescope's gaze. These two
figures further problematize any unitary resolution of
the novel's politics by introducing even more discourses and their claims of value – discourses of race,
power, wealth and poverty. Both figures represent
categories that the F-group has little concern for, and
that play no part of the narrator's erotic and romantic
ambitions.

The black tourist, as an American, as one enabled
to travel, as one standing on top of the mountain, is
associated with wealth and power. The only entry his
blackness makes into the category of racism comes
through the narrator's self-consciousness about having specified his colour, and her move throughout the
next few references to him toward naming him only
as "the tourist." Nevertheless, his colour operates to
qualify his position of power, to serve notice that it
is a winnable position, one only recently won. The
telescope he holds operates in another direction,

however, associating him with a long history of male dominance. It marks him, like the camera that Jon carries, as the specular man, the one whose gaze legitimizes female beauty, frames and defines reality, and extends the effective range of control and power.

Contrastingly without access to telescope, mountain or power is the grey woman who is constituted by the telescope's reach but powerless to look through it. She is the "grey" woman, without colour, without even the controversial blackness of the tourist. More marginal than he, more marginal than the anglophone narrator, "[t]he grey woman stands, her filthy skirt falling about her stained legs" (57). "Her shoulders shake and shake from coughing" (166). She is the ultimate version of *Heroine*'s excluded women – the revolutionary women who serve mainly as bedmates for the revolutionary men, the exploited waitresses, the young hookers, Polly the Mafia wife whose estranged husband's well-paid lawyers legally take her children from her, or the elderly steno who was exposed to so many alien forms of language throughout her career that now "everything that goes in her ears goes out her mouth" (43): "Political situation prostituting fascist referendum wife of *Frank's girl's legs mufflers getting expensive four-to-one the Expos under conditions for selling stocks on St James' the church over the bridge at skis in the oracle . . .*" (42).

The grey woman, like her sister who forgot to speak to her dentist, exists even further outside discourse, living alone on streets where no one may ever speak to her.

*

"You'll never be anything but a fellow traveller" . . .
"Why?" I asked in a small voice (my lip twisting like
Hers on the verandah) . . . "Because you're an artist.
The way you mother that little Chilean kid makes us
also think you have parenting ambitions. Tandis qu'un
vrai révolutionnaire appartient 100 pour cent au
groupe." (98)

G.S.'s concerns about what she "should" do as she,
like the grey woman, wanders the streets of Montreal,
and her recurrent preoccupation elsewhere about
whether she is loved sufficiently by Jon, or whether
she should have accepted Marie's lesbian advances,
might very well strike her F-group comrades as signs
of bourgeois-individualism, and possibly even lead a
"bourgeois-nationalist" to accuse her of granting inappropriate priority to the personal over the collective. This emphasis on the personal over the
collective, however, is as much a property of the novel
itself as of G.S. the character. Despite the concern it
shows in its "black" and "grey" frame characters
about systemic exploitations and exclusions, *Heroine*
gives by far most of its attention firstly to G.S.'s
individual relationship to Marxism, lesbianism, feminism and romantic idealism and secondly to how the
individual self is constituted and to the relative instability of this constitution. Even its portrayal of 1970s
Quebec is overshadowed by its concern with the way
in which G.S.'s hungry, desiring self is constructed,
reconstructed but never satisfied by the various dis-

cursive assertions she encounters. The only note of consistency the novel gives its first-person narrator is the anguish of her cry to Mama: "why'd you put this hole in me." Otherwise it presents her as a melange of names, lacks, phrases and ideologies. It shows her desperately needing the romantic exclusionary image she and Jon project as a "beautiful couple" (18) or "the perfect revolutionary couple" (16) while also feeling she must visibly reject monogamy in order to "improve [her] revolutionary image" (98). It shows her wanting also some distinct legitimacy among the F-group women as a radical feminist, and so writing and presenting the paper "The Issue of Equal Access to Sexuality for Women in Non-Monogamous Heterosexual Couples" (65) in a vain attempt to bridge both male and female interests. It has her name herself variously "G.S.," "I," "Gail," "widow" and "heroine." It has her seek advice from conflicting sources – from Jon, from the lesbian Marie, even from an anglophone psychiatrist at McGill University. Throughout most of her narration, the novel shows her lying in a bathtub, masturbating beneath the faucet, and both sorting her conflicting identities, desires and memories, and making various literary efforts to frame these for the novel she hopes to write. The flowing water from the faucet emphasizes the fluidity and mutability of her memories and viewpoints, while the enclosing tub emphasizes the paralysis of indecision that her life has reached.

The novel also works to discredit notions of unified subjectivity through G.S.'s changing views of other characters. On her arrival in Montreal, G.S.'s desperation to possess a unified self-image is paralleled by her projection of unity onto the people she meets. She perceives the "green-eyed girl" who is her main rival for Jon's affections as an archetypally jealous schemer who will deploy Marxist doctrine to discredit her or pose as a lesbian to conceal her own heterosexual designs. She sees Marie as the strong, decisive "new woman" and overlooks the ambivalent desire Marie's repeated visits to her suggest. She sees Jon as a hero, a teacher who will enable her to "learn of politics and culture" (18). His professional work as a photographer – he works as a wedding photographer by day and a revolutionary creator of social documents by night – increases his aura of authority: "Later, my love, taking pictures, when it seemed to me we saw it all the same, I began to think of you as an extra window on the world. Helping me figure out what real is" (40). She is consequently distressed when any of these characters behave inconsistently or in ways that imply disapproval of her. But, of course, within the novel itself they too are discursively constructed characters, who also experience the various discursive conflicts the various chapter titles encode: between romantic love and pragmatic reality ("Car Wrecks and Bleeding Hearts"), between self-sufficiency and social responsibility ("Free Woman and the Shadow in the Bank") and between creative independence and immersion in another ("I was a Poet before I was You").

Initially, the heroine that G.S. would construct of

herself as the protagonist of the novel she hopes to write is a woman who would meet all discursive expectations and transcend their contradictions. "Her goal is to maintain a certain (modern) equilibrium. To be on every front a totally avant-garde woman . . . Detachment is part of the image she's working on" (62). To some extent this heroine is a parody of the demands G.S. makes of herself in aspiring to be an emotionally-fulfilled lover, a Marxist revolutionary and a radical feminist. "Strong and passionate, her own person. Any pain she feels, she keeps hidden . . . So that the external image with the black leather jacket, handrolled cigarette and heavy eye makeup is impeccably courageous" (58). Later, even though the narrator allows her more latitude – "a heroine can be sad, distressed, it just has to be in a social context" (84) – she appears to be an idealization of the narrator:

I have to admit my mind also turned to my own slight lack [of a sex life]. And I said:

> "I'll never write a word untouched like this." But twas only a passing moment. The heroine wouldn't have this problem, having learned a certain flair (example: the way she combs her hair or wears a sweater) by coming up to Montreal. Yes, she views the *savoir-vivre* as a part of her struggle against whatever she hated back in Lively. This vision of a future where everyone is beautiful buoys her determination to live each day as the perfect revolutionary. Striving constantly to combine the political with the personal. (102)

Only when the narrator leaves her bathtub do she and

the heroine-persona begin to converge. "The heroine stands up. Drawing her blanket close, she takes the blue sheets and puts them on a violin stand beside the television. She steps back" (180). "Heroinism" at this point, however, no longer has political content; it has become merely an individual's "brave" attempt to continue to live – to leave a bathtub, or take a mundane walk outside one's home. "The heroine keeps walking" (181).

*

Heroine's emphasis on feminism and on a woman's subjective well-being is evident even in its narrative structure. As Marcia Blumberg has pointed out, *Heroine* consists of a 61-page section entitled "Beginning," an 8-page Section II, untitled, and a 100-page section III titled "Ending." Blumberg identifies this structure of substantial outer sections surrounding a slight centre as similar to the structure Toril Moi has noted in Luce Irigaray's *Speculum of the Other Woman* – "a hollow surface on the model of the speculum/vagina," "the centre . . . framed by the two massive sections" (Blumberg 58; Moi 130). The overall text of *Heroine* would appear to be a gynaecological rejoinder to the Phallus and patriarchy, and an assertion of the priority of gender politics over both national and other transnational ones. The phallus itself, together with Jon's powerful camera, is reduced by *Heroine* to a "single eye" (9), a sadly specular water faucet that G.S. controls not to penetrate her vagina but to spurt "warmly over [her] uh small point" (36), to "stay warm as [a] sperm river" (126).

Neither Canada nor Quebec have large roles in the imagination of *Heroine*. English-Canada is a place of banishment when the F-Group is warned by the police to go there during the Olympic Games; Quebec, at first glance, is an exotic foretaste of international culture and avant-garde politics – a place that becomes, however, much less exotic once the condition of women within it becomes evident. The official politics of both Canada and Quebec are dismissed by *Heroine* as regressive – as protecting bourgeois materialism by exploiting the weak, especially women like the "grey" lady or the elderly stenographer. What engages the novel's imagination is not a feminism within national politics but a transnational feminism. This feminism seeks action rather than essence, envisions socially situated expansions of women's fields of action: greater choice of discourses, larger spaces in which to write one's own script, or construct one's own heroine; enlarged space for this heroine to walk out into any city's "grey light, . . . standing on the sidewalk . . . her pale red curls her one sign of beauty" (183).

NOTES

1   This essay is a slightly edited version of a chapter of Frank Davey's *Post-National Arguments: The Politics of the Anglophone-Canadian Novel since 1967* (Toronto: U of Toronto P, 1993) 210-222. Reprinted with permission of the publishers.

WORKS CITED

Blumberg, Marcia. "Rereading Gail Scott's *Heroine*: A Triple Lens of Sighting/Citing/Siting." *Open Letter* 8.2 (Winter 1992): 57-69.

Irigaray, Luce. *Speculum of the Other Woman*. 1974. Trans. Gillian G. Gill. Ithaca: Cornell UP, 1985.

McCrea, Mary. *Montreal Magic*. Montreal: Optimum, 1982.

Moi, Toril. *Sexual/Textual Politics*. 1985. London: Routledge, 1988.

Scott, Gail. *Heroine*. Toronto: Coach House, 1987.

Femme(s) Focale(s): Main Brides and the Post-identity Narrative

JENNIFER HENDERSON

Gail Scott's second novel can be read as a text that displaces the narrative quest(ion) for/of identity.[1] In *Main Brides*, identities, rather than being discovered in a plumbing of depths, are the effects of a fantasizing production which takes place at the level of focalization. Truth as depth, as expressive inner essence, is reformulated as a fantasy spun from a reading of surfaces. The text reverses the traditional location of value in the depth/surface opposition, and surface is newly valued as the side providing possibilities for self-invention, movement and hope for women in a social context of rampant misogynist violence. This de-ontologizing reversal has consequences for narrative structure: the quest structure that fixes gender identities is replaced in *Main Brides* with "concentric constellations" of shifting identities (Scott 110).[2]

With a gaze that takes in the corporeal surfaces of other women – gestures, flashes of skin, ornamentation, various modes of self-styling – a *femme focale* produces fantasized inner depths for other women passing through her space in a bar-café on Montreal's boulevard St. Laurent, otherwise known as The Main. This gaze belongs to Lydia, a character who is only made accessible to us through portraits of other women which she fabricates from intriguing surface details. Nothing "happens" in this novel, for Lydia's only movement is her slippage in and out of identifications with these women as she waits out an afternoon and evening sipping wine, trying to recover from the shock of spotting a girl's corpse in the park at the beginning of her day. Lydia's portraits – fantasies of who the other women might be, weighted with memory and desire – blur the distinctions between perception and imagination, self and other, so that it is often unclear whether the subject of the portrait is the other woman or a projection of Lydia herself. The discrete identities which are necessary to a dialectical resurrection of the boundaries of a (male) self after a passage through (female) otherness give way to an organizing principle of porosity. The only possible candidate for central point of reference – Lydia, the agent of the look – is an unanchored centre, without a proper identity.

We encounter Lydia as the anonymous pair of eyes through which the first scene of the frame narrative unfolds. Not long afterwards, this internal focalization through Lydia switches to external focalization on her:

> The woman (her name is Lydia) stares out the window. Occasional clients might confuse her with a Portugese woman, slightly older. Who comes in every day, keys twirling, waiting for her lover. Ele-

gant in a European way. Dressed in crisp white blouse,
slim skirt, like Lydia. Who (at 39) is already a little out
of fashion. Compared to the students parading down
the sidewalk. (31)

As seen through the eyes of other patrons, Lydia is an
object distinguishable through the same details of
vesture – "crisp white blouse, slim skirt" – which
permit her to be confused with another woman,
"Portugese." Lydia's identity is a permanently unset-
tled question. The text maintains a caginess around
the issue of her ethnicity, in revealing/concealing
descriptions such as the following: "her eye (traced
with a curved line of black, particularly decisive at the
outer corner like on a Greek frieze, indicating the
strain of Mediterranean in her)" – where there is no
assurance of a real ethnicity underneath the makeup
which copies a Mediterranean look (132). The nature
of her desire is also uncertain, as the narrative discourse acknowledges: "What she did for sex? True,
it went missing from the facts" (167). There are
indications that she has desired both men and
women: confusingly, whilst still dressing in "purple
clothes," she was an advocate of "loving women"
and yet, in the present of the text, looking "like
someone from a Simone de Beauvoir novel," "only
hat[ing] the stockings," she *intends* to become a
lesbian (147, 158, 138, 32).

Lydia does not acquire depth and solidity as the
result of excursions into otherness but is, rather,
dispersed in her fantasized portraits of other women.
The vertical seepage between layered focalizing per-

spectives is doubled by a porosity along the horizontal axis of the text, in uncanny reappearances of phrases from one portrait to the next. A move such as "walk[ing] over to the phone and putt[ing] a quarter in. Trying not to sound desperate" is repeated in multiple contexts; likewise, kicking back a chair is a gesture that is resignified at various points across the space of the text with the repetition/dislocation of Derridean *différance*. The revenge attack of which one woman dreams is carried out many portraits later – seemingly with the same weapon – by a different woman, not as an act of revenge but of self-defense. Lydia is not the sovereign source of these fantasized narrative fragments but, rather, a point of refraction in a field of signifying bodies/surfaces, a re-reader of "tropes" circulating in the bar – configurations of cultural, linguistic, sexual and gender signs which are already readings of other texts. There is Norma Jean, for instance, modelling a self on Marilyn Monroe, an icon that is already "a trope for something currently in the air" – or Z. the drag artist, a "woman in some ways impossible to grasp . . . Always appearing in ambivalent and parsimonious fragments" (181, 136). Lydia, too, is a text and not an originary consciousness, a relational subject-*effect* functioning as a focalizing perspective.

*

As point of entry to this analysis, I offer a symptomatic reading of a *Globe and Mail* review. My purpose is not to preface a correct reading of *Main Brides* with a misreading, but rather to draw upon the productive encounter of an old horizon with some new terrain. The "old" in this case is a perspective that looks for ontological certainty in narrative, a perspective which is bound to be frustrated by Scott's reworking of the narrative grammar in which truths and identities are produced. Scott's first move is to refuse to represent a transcendental subject capable of serving as the source of meaning. The lack of such a sovereign and determining perspective in *Main Brides* troubles the *Globe and Mail*'s reviewer:

> Scott's framing device – imagined lives – works against her in the long run. The reader puzzles over how much these are independent representations (was Nanette really in the park? Was there a flasher?), how much Lydia's slightly soused musings. In either case, the method undercuts the author's and narrator's commitment to the characters, and not even a bit of postmodernist, self-referential razzle-dazzle will rescue us. (Persky C13)

What this reader desires to be rescued from is uncertainty as to the status of the narrative discourse. He must decide whether the portraits are inside or outside the frame narrative (the sections of the text entitled "the sky is what I want"), whether meaning is produced by an unreliable character (Lydia) or guaranteed by a sober, independent source. In these dilemmas I propose that we read the sighting of something important within an oversight. The reviewer's hesitation points to a question that is not in fact posed in his review: *Is* this a narrative designed to satisfy the desire to know, a narrative which proceeds toward truth by a peeling away of surfaces? In the epistemological regime of the hermeneutic narrative, identity is an ontological category; however, in *Main Brides*, identities are produced as unstable, discontinuous, contingent surface effects. The "pediment" of the text's subtitle (*Against Ochre Pediment and Aztec Sky*) is an emblem for its concern with ornamental truths: a decoration crowning the top of a building, the pediment is a fake because, like all the identities in this text, it has no depth. In *Main Brides*, even the cat is a "little fake" (182).

Scott's text plays allusively with a narrative genre organized around the gradual elimination of hesitation, the establishment of the truth-value of witnesses' discourse and the desire to know absolutely "what was really." The detective story would perhaps be the logical route for a narrative instigated, as is *Main Brides*, by the sighting in a park of a "lumpy shadow, with [a] blanket thrown over it" (61). However, Lydia prefers the *dérive* of drunken "voyeurism" (Scott, "Interview" 4) to the fact-checking of detective work and the narrative takes a course in which "the 'line' of reason breaks [and] a person can do anything. Take in any number of impressions" (16). The detective story that would solve the mystery of the murdered woman in the park thus remains an evoked absence, an explicitly evaded route. In the narratological lexicon proposed by Gérard Genette, the missing detective story in *Main Brides* constitutes a *paralipsis* – an omission of information that is "necessary in principle" within the focalizing frame; the fantasized portraits substituted for that story constitute the opposite type of infraction, *paralepses*, which give "information that should be left aside" (195). Genette reserves these terms for "isolated infractions" of a dominant, "coherent" organization of focalization (195). In the case of *Main Brides*, "infraction" is the rule: a paraliptical frame narrative, circling around an omitted detective story, alternates with paraleptical narrative fragments swerving off in unpredictable, implausible directions.

The genre of the detective story (present in this text through its marked absence) figures the kind of reading – and the conception of knowledge that goes along with it – that is troubled by *Main Brides*. If the question of truth commits the one who wants to know to a search for the ultimate source of meaning, that source proves to be unlocatable in a text working to produce hesitation rather than certainty. A hesitating reader is represented within the text itself, in Lydia, whose fantasizing activity allows her to enter the scenarios she produces. Lydia is rarely in control of the boundaries between inside and outside, self and other, which would secure for her the distanced position of a voyeur. When she slips into these narrative fragments the usual distinction between focalizing subject and focalized object is blurred and a fantasized subject that is/is not Lydia is produced. The effacement of limits between self and other is a characteristic theme of the pole of fantastic literature

retrieves the (albeit fragmented) story of the other woman in the bar. A fantasized identity is thus set up as the *source* of surface signification. However, *Main Brides* also unveils this fiction of unveiling. Lydia points to it, in the case of Nanette, as an unsuccessful aesthetic technique; in the portrait of Z., both the red-head in the bar and the referent of nostalgia are shown to be outer husks and the search for a self-identical core turns up only a discontinuous chain of signifiers. The recollected Z. is already a trace, a stylization, a shifting image like the pink flamingo in the window across the street from the bar, which seems to have shifted every time it catches Lydia's eye. If the process of knowledge-constitution involves possessing the object once the veil is lifted, this process is foiled when, like Z., the girl-object proves to be an infinitude of veils, "impossible to grasp" (136).

The process involved in empirical knowing is a kind of narrative – the narrative of a subject's encounter with an object. We thus return to the missing detective story in *Main Brides*, for the genre which this text evokes and evades consists precisely in a narrativization of true knowing. The subject of empiricist knowledge *par excellence*, a detective comes up against the obstacle of false appearances in his search for truth; he eliminates that obstacle "by a whole series of sortings, sievings, scrapings and rubbings" (Althusser 36). If de Lauretis is right, we should add penetrations to that list, for the obstacle is always on the other side of the pole of *sexual difference* – and the process of discovery in which it is conquered by a masculine hero is the Oedipally structured narrative. In her feminist-structuralist analysis of the narrative form, de Lauretis argues that the boundary through which every hero must pass along the path toward the accomplishment of his identity marks the place of the non-man, the monster, the female in the topography of narrative. Every narrative is essentially a quest in which a hero "encounters [obstacles] on the path of life, on his way to manhood, wisdom, and power; they must be slain or defeated so that he can go forward to fulfil his destiny – and his story" (110). The specific threat posed by the original feminized obstacle (the Sphinx, the Medusa) is a threat to man's *vision*. Here, then, is the meeting point of the obstacle in narrative and the husk in the empiricist model of knowledge, both impediments to vision: vision in the literal sense, vision in the philosophical sense of knowledge, and vision as trope for phallic agency. Just as the object of empirical knowledge is constituted by an operation which passes through its inessential part, (masculine) identity is constituted in narrative in the hero's act of conquering an obstacle. Only after prevailing over the she-monster, penetrating the outer husk, does the hero (or the empirically-minded detective) arrive at his destination.

Taking the myth of Oedipus as her model, de Lauretis argues that narrative destination is an answer to the question of identity. Narrative is structured as a quest(ion) prompted by the desire to know – and the desire to know woman in particular (111). This theory of narrative form concurs with the logico-semiotic theory proposed by Greimas, in which a "deep grammar" is anthropomorphized and converted in the surface narrative grammar into the movement of a subject toward an object. De Lauretis shares Greimas's sense of a deep structure of oppositions underneath a narrative surface. Up to a point, her theory of narrative does not seem to have any argument with the polar logic of the empiricist conception of knowledge; in fact, it deploys the same oppositions – depth/surface, inside/outside, active/passive, passage/boundary, subject/object.[4] She sees sexual difference as constitutive of this series of oppositions and argues that male identity is made and remade in the narrative quest in the passage through female otherness. But what if a narrative neither takes a linear, interrogative form nor relies on the subject-object relation? What would a narrative look like if sexual identity were not discovered at the end of a quest(ion), but performed or continually reinvented?

Main Brides troubles the notions of causality which underpin the concept of a deep structure moving in linear fashion towards a surface manifestation in language. In Genette's lexicon, story is the name of this deep core, the "signified or narrative content" presumed to exist prior to the "signifier, statement, discourse or narrative text itself" (27). *Fabula* is the term Mieke Bal borrows from the Russian formalists for the narrative bedrock that she describes as a "logic of events" with a homological relation to "connected series of human actions" in the "extra-literary" world (12-13). In this hypothetical raw material of narrative, events occur in chronological order at an invariable pace and relationships between elements are "necessary," not yet "symbolic, allusive, etc." (7). The *fabula* is understood to be prior to the processes of arrangement and ordering through which it is transformed, at the next level, into a story, and then, finally, with the addition of linguistic signs at the uppermost level, into a narrative text (7-8). When the structuralist horizon is replaced by one in which signs are seen to refer not to a prediscursive narrative content but, rather, to other signs, the premise of a *fabula* can no longer serve as the foundation of narrative.

Scott's text favours the "crooked line" (Z.'s sign), the "zigzag" of Lydia's inebriated step into the night at the end, signifying surfaces bouncing off one another (151, 228). It is the narrative discourse itself – the final, uppermost layer, in the terms of structuralist narratology – which operates as the (non-original) source of signification. Shifting nomenclatures and modes of address, a sometimes ambiguous use of the pronoun she, and the shuffling-together of different verbal tenses produce events at the level of discourse. Linkages are effected through processes of repetition and metonymic accretion in an "ontology of accidental attributes" (Butler 24). The red tunic of a Kingston officer-boyfriend is pastiched by a red suit-jacket in the same portrait before turning up in a later portrait in the form of the red A-line coat which gives away the Ontarian in Montréal. Also floating across the text is the cowgirl attire that is initially the *gauche* look of an Albertan lover but turns up again and again on other women in details such as a check shirt, and the images of seductive "horsewomen" in the background of a performance piece. Relations of *différance* – replacing the logic of cause-and-effect, the syntax of the predicative sentence – construct a plural, im-proper narrative form: an *"Installation with Muddy Frames"* (the idea for a book of portraits which is stolen from Lydia by a Toronto artist) (181). Instead of taking the form of a linear quest, then, narrative opens into identity-confusing "concentric constellations" – to use the text's figure for female orgasm (110). Such *mise en abymes* for its own reshaping of narrative form proliferate throughout the text. This reshaping is involved in a larger project of producing public images of alternative desiring positions, in the interest of the new kind of history that Lydia describes as "smooth and gently moving (her hand makes a wavy motion in the air)" (199).

Once the *fabula* has become a theoretical impossibility, focalization – that supposedly secondary operation converting a deep structure into a narrative text – becomes a much more prominent aspect of signification: a mode of seeing which supplements what is seen. In the text's first demonstration of *productive* focalization, Lydia's gaze effects a re-signification of the privileged sign of heterosexual and patriarchal ideology, the bridal portrait. In the opening section of the frame narrative, Lydia's glance takes in the image of a bride in the window of a Portugese photo store (9). When the image is repeated twenty-

six pages later, the bride has been cut out of the
context in which she was the "Main thing in the
picture for a single minute of her life" and pasted up
against the sky with the pediments crowning the tops
of buildings (10). Here, she is a *permanently* fascinating woman, the first rebellious "woman-on-the-roof"
to be created by Lydia's confusion of perception and
imagination. Lydia's focalization does not consist in
showing positive phenomena from a particular, restricted point of view but, rather, in constituting its
very objects. The cutting and pasting which re-signi-
fies the bridal image – making the image of an unknown woman a fascinating surface, a kind of
heraldic sign – gets expanded in Lydia's narrativized
portraits of women in the bar. Spinning off corporeal
surfaces in her fantasizing focalization, Lydia inserts
them in narrative fragments which blur the distinctions between real, imagined and remembered, and
between self and other.

In this post-structuralist approach to focalization
the focalizer herself also ceases to be a sovereign,
self-determining subject: "Lydia *(the portrait)*" is an
intertextual construct producing other texts in her
reading of surfaces (197; emphasis added). In the
terms that *Main Brides* proposes, subjectivity is an
extreme form of receptivity and porosity: "[a]n omen
of sensations reassur[es] Lydia she's reached the real
state of detachment, when one finally becomes a
person. Free enough to take in all exterior impressions" (132). The ambiguous activity/passivity of this
"taking in" brings us back to the fantasmatic configu-

ration in which the subject, not quite in control of the staging, gets "caught up" in a sequence. When it comes to "knowing who is responsible for the setting" of this sequence, Laplanche and Pontalis hand their psychoanalytic account of fantasy over to philosophy (27), but perhaps the question of who directs the scene is one to be worked out by post-structuralist feminist narratology. It is with this in mind that I return now to de Lauretis, in order to see how her theory of focalization would have to be adjusted to accommodate the layered, fantasized mode of focalization of *Main Brides*.

Despite the structuralist emphasis of "Desire in Narrative," de Lauretis's essay does not assign a secondary role to focalization. De Lauretis's interest in the *filmic* text permits her to consider the productive work of point of view, and the ways in which the camera articulates a "vision *for* the spectator" in classical Hollywood cinema, even *producing* the spectator "as Oedipus, male subject, restoring to him . . . a vision capable of exciting desire for" the image of woman (148). The production of the female spectator is more complicated. De Lauretis builds a theory of the duplicitous and contradictory positioning of the female spectator through an analysis of the play of identification in Hitchcock's *Rebecca*. The specular structure of this film involves both the diegetic image of a woman (a heroine) and an intradiegetic image, the portrait of a woman with whom the heroine identifies and whom the heroine also comes to *desire* in her capacity as protagonist. For the spectator, then, the heroine is a point of identification capable of "sustaining the oscillation between 'femininity' and 'masculinity'" – between what de Lauretis calls the passive "woman position" in the topography of narrative and the Oedipal, desiring position, the "figure of narrative movement" (152, 144). The heroine with whom the spectator identifies does not just want to be the woman in the portrait, she also *wants* the woman in the portrait; identification with her position, therefore, involves the spectator in a productive confusion. What this reading of *Rebecca*'s specular structure contributes to the question of focalization is a problematization of the female spectator's (or reader's) identification with the "single image" of a "true" woman in a text (de Lauretis 155). However, de Lauretis's scheme not only sticks to binary frames – the principle of contradiction still relies on such oppositions as active/passive, having/being, masculine/feminine – but also fails to imagine the possibility of a narrative *not* organized as (Oedipal) quest, with a subject pursuing an object and securing an identity in the process. How would focalization work in a narrative in which identities were not discovered as truths, but acted out?

The "concentric constellations" of *Main Brides* involve multiple intradiegetic images of women whose cores are constructed in a fantasizing reading of corporeal surfaces. They are produced as contingent, accidental effects – furthermore, not as static landscapes but, rather, as narrativized portraits. The subject of the portrait is *herself* a figure of narrative movement. Lydia's relation to the subjects of these portraits consists neither in an identification that consolidates a sense of self (the "feminine," passive side of de Lauretis's contradictory positioning) nor in a desire for possession (the "masculine" side). The relation is modelled, rather, on the fantasmatic configuration in which the external object is abandoned and desire is articulated in an auto-hypnotic, auto-erotic *mise-en-scène*. The fantasizing subject

> forms no representation of the desired object but is [her]self represented as participating in the scene although . . . [she] cannot be assigned any fixed place in it . . . As a result, the subject, although always present in the fantasy, may be so in a desubjectivized form, that is to say, in the very *syntax* of the sequence in question. (Laplanche and Pontalis 26; emphasis added)

Lydia's presence in some portraits is discernable *only* as a layer of focalization, showing itself in the occasional appearance of details from the context of the frame narrative. These portraits in which Lydia no longer makes an appearance as a remembering subject are more purely modelled along the lines of fantasy. Her focalizing perspective slides underneath another perspective which it, in fact, produces, and then gets carried away. We move into the third portrait, "Dis-May," by way of Lydia's imaginative musing at the end of a section of frame narrative in the bar on The Main. With her gaze fixed on a stranger whom she calls "the *mambo*-dancing woman" (because of her evident taste for Latin music), Lydia imagines this woman on vacation in Cuba. Soon "it's too late to stop" and the imagined transposition is suddenly achieved as the text cuts from the scene of the frame narrative to that of fantasy (66-67). "*Mambo!*" – the first line of the portrait – is the metonymic sign through which the text leaps into Cuba; instead of a cause-and-effect sequence, it is an accidental detail – the tape being played in the bar – which motivates this cut. The word *mambo*, in fact, punctuates the entire portrait, resonating in multiple directions: it is a warning sounded with each resurfacing of the memory of rape which the woman is trying to forget (in a doubling of Lydia's willed amnesia regarding the murdered body in the park); *mambo* is also the dance movement which this woman tries to pick up as a ritual of forgetting. "*Mam-bo*. Because you have to lighten up"; "[t]o get over trauma you just need to keep moving. *One-two, one-two*" (77, 85). But it also functions as a trace of Lydia in the bar where the *mambo* tape is playing, quilting together the focalizing perspectives of Lydia in Montréal and "the *mambo*-dancing woman" in Cuba and indicating that Lydia is present, somewhere, everywhere, in the sequence of images.

The portrait ends with the "*mambo*-dancing woman's" realization that she has lost her "little sister"-companion,[5] possibly to a tidal wave, in a moment of distraction on the beach. "You step forward. Look behind. My god where is she?" (95). This moment occurs at the very end of the portrait, on the brink of a cut back to Lydia in the bar. If this were a shot-reverse shot sequence in a classical realist film, the terrified "[l]ook behind" would be followed by the reverse shot of a tidal wave carrying away the "sister." The shot-reverse shot sequence in film is designed to create the illusion of spatial coherence on screen, by matching a character's gaze with that which she "sees." But in Scott's text, the reverse shot gives us Lydia in the bar, instead of the horrifying image which produces the "*mambo*-dancing woman's" horrified reaction. The first line of this return to the frame narrative reads, "What if she screamed out loud? Lydia looks, embarrassed, around the bar," as if Lydia *herself* were reacting to the sight of the "sister" being swept away (96). The reverse shot is thus of another "seer," instead of a picture of what is seen. This play with the "eyeline match" convention of realist film coordinates the "*mambo*-dancing woman's" gaze with another gaze that is supposedly outside the space of the portrait. As the palimpsest shifts, the space outside is revealed to be inside, a layer of focalization.

Lydia's "embarrassing" scream resembles the re-action of the naïve film spectator whose suturing with a character on screen is so seamless as to permit a full integration into the filmic fiction. In such suturings the spectator loses awareness of the immediate spectating situation and forgets her self. But as Lydia scrambles to re-assemble a coherent self after her scream, the reader, too, must regain footing, for the second-person address of the "Dis-May" portrait collapses the reader with the "you" of the portrait. When the reaction to what is seen by "you" on the beach is taken on by *Lydia*, then, the reader is implicated in a palimpsest of different focalizing perspectives, "caught up" – through the "you" of the portrait, through Lydia – in a concentric framework of points of view. Lydia, the fantasized *"mambo*-dancing woman," and the reader are subjects of the same surprised look – a situation which returns us to the question which troubled the *Globe and Mail* reviewer and caused Laplanche and Pontalis to hand the theorization of fantasy over to philosophy: Who directs the fantasy-narrative?

Interpellated by the second-person address of the "Dis-May" portrait, the reader appears to be slotted, along with the other woman in the bar, into a sequence of actions controlled by Lydia's fantasizing focalization. And as in the only other portrait to be narrated in the second person, the "you" of "Dis-May" marks a lesbian desiring position. In sentences such as "You stare at the darker of the two . . . imagining her preference," then, the reader gazes with/as a lesbian subject, apparently through the agency of Lydia (81). But Lydia's involuntary scream at the end of the portrait demonstrates that the narrative is not entirely within her control: she, herself, is swept away by the sequence of images. There is, then, no controlling position outside of this constellation of lesbian looks: the gaze which Lydia projects in fantasy is capable of surprising her. It can also turn back to face her, as the portrait entitled "Donkey

Riding" demonstrates. This time, the subject of the portrait is an *intra*subjective other, a projection of Lydia's anglo and, it appears, sexually abused self, who will refuse the self/other distinction that Lydia has tried to maintain. Norma jean beats Lydia at her own game: as it turns out, she knows Lydia better than Lydia knows her(self). "[G]lancing ironically at Lydia," this projected version of an old, painful part of the self reads in the fragmented notes which have slipped out of Lydia's hand "'*The Perfect Incest Dream*'" (196).

*

A detective of sorts, the *Globe and Mail* reviewer of *Main Brides* reads for depth; like the structuralist narratologist, he looks for a recognizable logic of events beneath the surface of the narrative text. The search does not prove satisfying but, again, the (non)findings are instructive, for the marking of the text's studied superficiality draws in an important, related issue:

> True, most of Scott's linked-tales carry an undertone of dread, reverberations of the violence experienced especially by women in contemporary society. It's also unfortunately true that not much happens in these stories, either in terms of plot or by way of a developing depth of language or feeling. (C13)

"Unfortunately true" here are both the pervasive threats of violence "especially" against women in our

society and the lack of depth in the narrative fragments of *Main Brides*. The reviewer unwittingly
draws a connection here which touches on the text's
feminist politics of surfaces – "exterior impressions"
(132) – a politics that brings together a re-thinking of
identity in terms of performative production and a
concern with women's "(material) capacity for existence" in a social context of incest, rape and – what is
impossible to forget in a text set in Montreal in the
1990s – femicide (199). The theme of violence does
indeed make its way into each of the portraits,
whether it takes the form of a stalking stranger, the
clenched fist of a homophobe, a father's hand or "the
damned lumpy shadow, with . . . blanket thrown over
it" that Lydia is trying to forget (61). But Scott moves
the theme of violence away from the genre of the
survivor story, the personal story of pain operated by
an epistemic/ontological regime that constructs and
reifies identities such as that of "Incest survivor.
Victim" – locking women into the "rigid, even homi-
cidal" history from which they would escape (199,
135). *Main Brides* reserves the language of depth for
the description of symptoms of a past trauma in
Lydia: a "huge solid mass like a giant turd trying to
come out of the top of her head" (187). But Lydia
fights against the consolation for such inner discomfort that might be found in a retreat into the "MOI"
(162), the fearful, defensive stasis of a project of
recovery which would attach her to a rigorously
interior and anterior, pre-social identity. How can
women resist the pressure to fix as deep truth the

"inner anguish under" that comes from memories of incest and rape or the everyday experience of misogynist violence (130)? Lydia's trick is to find a "state of somnambulism-*almost*: head in the clouds, feet on the ground. Which state permits enlargement of exterior perception without interior disturbance" (100; emphasis added). In interview, Scott has called this state a "parenthesis" between writing and renewed (self)creation (4).

Judith Butler suggests that feminists look for a source of agency not in I-narratives anchoring inner cores, but in a material production of identities using the body as an aesthetic surface. In this alternate survival strategy, "in and through the complex cultural exchanges among bodies, . . . identity itself is ever-shifting, . . . constructed, disintegrated, and re-circulated in a dynamic field of cultural relations" (127). Butler's theory of the performative production of identity learns from a history of theorizing about performative utterances but, also, from the drag artist's playful engagement with culturally-regulated gender identities. The drag artist, as she notes, is a specialist in the re-signification of gender: a "spectre of discontinuity and incoherence" who dislodges the norms of intelligibility through which sexual identity is constituted as a prediscursive, biological sex expressed in gender (and in the sexuality that flows "naturally" from that gender) (17). The figure of Z. in *Main Brides* is just such an incoherent configuration of signs, a perfectly-bilingual "kind of emaciated drag queen," "lesbienne," "guru," "Pierrot-like" performance artist, "Female junkie. *Vogue* model. Pisces woman. Aging punk" (142, 149, 146, 140, 139). Always "sampling" popular culture in her corporeal signification, Z. substitutes the "crooked line" for the continuous line of the expressive model of identity; Z.'s sign suspends the origin. But besides Z. there is also Adèle, the train-travelling subject of the second portrait, whose officer-chasing is part of an anachronistic self-styling that mimics an obsession more legitimate in a nineteenth-century woman. Always on the move "in the many layers of clothing of a woman who travels light," she refuses to be proper to her time and place (42). And, of course, Lydia herself is "one of those people you meet travelling. Who feels better in another language. Spending hours in her room dressing up 'to pass' " (53).

As stultifying as the gender identity reinforced by the structure of classical narrative are constructions of the self based on "withdrawal[s] into a kind of egotism. I.e., . . . strong identifying narrative[s]" (162), including those of victim, bride, anglo, heterosexual. As a portrait of Lydia herself, then, the text offers *nothing but* props, substitutes, projections, displacements – a constant troping. Lydia is (constituted in) an activity of re-reading the corporeal surfaces of others. If, as Butler writes, gender is a "cultural/corporeal action that requires a new vocabulary," it also requires a new reading practice, of the kind represented in Lydia's fantasizing focalization (12). We have seen how any conception of knowledge entails a process of discovery (a method of reading) that prepares the mold for the object of knowledge, shaping it in advance. If we are going to do away with the metaphysic of inner cores that postulates a prediscursive sex or a pretextual "logic of actions," something like Lydia's fascinated gaze – de-ontologizing in its narrativization of surfaces, swept away by the very sequences it imagines – might serve as a model of socio-textual reading. And, as a way of "[l]ooking for allusions, that is, attractive surface-images providing information on how to make an art out of [life]," a source of creative agency (55).

NOTES

1   This essay was originally published in a slightly longer version in *Studies in Canadian Literature/ Études en littérature canadienne* 20.1 (1995): 93-114.

2   Unless otherwise indicated, all Scott citations are from *Main Brides*.

3   Gayatri Chakravorty Spivak uses the rhetorical term *metalepsis* to name the operation by which a "subject-effect" is posited as sovereign cause in "Subaltern Studies: Deconstructing Historiography," *In Other Worlds: Essays in Cultural Politics* (New York; London: Routledge, 1987): 204-205.

4   Up to a point, because towards the end of "Desire in Narrative," when de Lauretis considers the position of the female film spectator, things loosen up and there is at least room for theorizing the productivity of a contradictory positioning.

5   This hyphenated nomination is necessitated by the ambiguity of the relationship between the two women in the "Dis-May" portrait – "you" and "your sister. Not your real sister. But that's another story" (71). The two are *passing* as sisters on their Cuban vacation.

WORKS CITED

Althusser, Louis, and Étienne Balibar. *Reading Capital*. Trans. Ben Brewster. London: Verso, 1979.

Bal, Mieke. *Narratology: Introduction to the Theory of Narrative*. Trans. Christine van Boheemen. Toronto: U of Toronto P, 1985.

Butler, Judith. *Gender Trouble: Feminism and the Subversion of Identity*. New York; London: Routledge, 1990.

de Lauretis, Teresa. *Alice Doesn't: Feminism, Semiotics, Cinema*. Bloomington: Indiana UP, 1984.

Derrida, Jacques. *Writing and Difference*. Trans. Alan Bass. Chicago: U of Chicago P, 1978.

Genette, Gérard. *Narrative Discourse: An Essay in Method*. Trans. Jane E. Lewin. Ithaca: Cornell UP, 1980.

Greimas, A. J. *On Meaning: Selected Writings in Semiotic Theory*. Trans. Paul J. Perron and Frank H. Collins. Theory and History of Literature. Vol. 38. Minneapolis: U of Minnesota P, 1987.

Laplanche, Jean, and Jean-Bertrand Pontalis. "Fantasy and the Origins of Sexuality." *Formations of Fantasy*. Ed. Victor Burgin, James Donald and Cora Kaplan. London; New York: Methuen, 1986. 5-34.

Persky, Stan. "Scenes from a Montreal café." Rev. of *Main Brides*, by Gail Scott. *Globe and Mail* 3 Jul. 1993: C13.

Scott, Gail. "Interview with Gail Scott." By Beverley Daurio. *Paragraph* 15.2 (Fall 1993): 3-7.

——. *Main Brides*. Toronto: Coach House, 1993.

The Nadja and Nanette of Gail Scott's *Main Brides* (*Against Ochre Pediment and Aztec Sky*)

CARLA HARRYMAN

We are surrounded by millennial discourses, both apocalyptic and utopian; medical science and technology promise us ever-greater control over birth, health, disease, and death, and promote an ethics of perfection reminiscent of late-nineteenth-century eugenic discourse.[1] At the same time we are in the throes of confusion and conflict over what is often described in terms of plague as we watch the spread of AIDS both within and outside of what at first seem to be contained communities. While projective statistics (for 1991, for 2000) force us into *fin-de-siècle* imagining, the churches, communities, and states struggle over how to support and maintain those already suffering. And this is to limit examples of millennial thinking to the sphere of the lived body – healthy or ill.

Frances Bartkowski, *Feminist Utopias*

[T]here is in young people and in erotic personalities throughout their lives a kind of intransitive mental feeling of being-in-love, which its objects only enter retrospectively; they were not given narcissistically in advance of this being-in-love either, that is, in their own body. Thus there is – not as a mental feeling, but rather as a state of mind – a light-heartedness of character, even hope; it certainly does not only appear when it knows clearly what it is hoping for.

Ernst Bloch, *The Principal of Hope*

In Gail Scott's *Main Brides*, the aesthetic is not perfect (it does not locate a millennial narrative as the site of utopian desire): "She thinks: 'it would be like reading a really embarrassing passage from my diary out loud.' That one about *Shiny Genitals*. Of course, it depends on how you handle it" (97). There is, however, a formulation of love, or desire, call it what one will, that in this work seeks the aesthetic and looks toward (*a forward feeling* – Bloch) a future *outside* the text.

The event of the novel, if one were to call it a novel (Scott originally wanted to call it "an installation"), occurs in a particular but not contained community, Montreal. The "characters" can be read as both aesthetic constructions (portraits written/drawn within the event of the novel) and hypothetical people, people who might exist and who might be able to affect the future as female subjects. In *Main Brides*, the anticipatory state is also a participatory state. Within its region are women subjects who individually and collectively practice becoming the subjects (even of their own participatory "self" objectifying) of a world in which the aesthetic signs of the culture, whether they created and instituted these signs/architectures or not, predominate as sites of engagement *for* them: "She glances up at the crookedly drawn 1904 pressed out of the metal ochre-colored roof-trim across the street. Remembering the times she let it unaesthetically hang out all over. Being too direct (example: in the portrait of Nanette)" (97). In *Main Brides* the doing and undoing and redoing of the particular community is in an active relationship to the already given, the already known.

In this way, the particular community is the opposite of a contained community. The concept of a contained community negates the differences between people and what use they make of their habitat or how a face or skirt can call attention to an elsewhere: "it isn't a crime to make up portraits of patrons in a bar (eavesdrop a little). She looks around discreetly" (the middle-aged Lydia is a little femme); "the Portuguese woman in white blouse and dark skirt, like hers, is getting up to try her phone call again" (97). Lydia's is a particular community – comprised of gay, lesbian, bisexual, straight people, dark people, immigrant people – that certain fearful discourses, such as those promulgated in mass media targeting suburbanites who identify with cities as scary places, might construct as *contained* communities in a narrative that addresses itself to people it supposes not to live there. The narrative about the contained community (for example, the scary urban environment with Queers and Quebecois) is one that presumes itself to be outside that which it narrates: it tells a story that institutes a millennial state of mind and encourages fear, hatred, and violent attacks, such as those against the young women students at Université de Montréal in 1991, an event which influenced Scott's novel.

André Breton and then later Alain Robbe-Grillet hold in contempt what they identify in the nine-teenth-century novel as a static and bankrupt literary psychology in which physical attributes of people and the objects that surround them are both class markers and reflections of states of mind (Breton, *Manifestoes of Surrealism* 6-9; see Robbe-Grillet's *For a New Novel*). Breton wanted to transform this static state through a method that chose interiority turned in-side-out into the world as the initiatory, not reflec-tive, site of human transformation. Robbe-Grillet wanted to revolutionize the novel, using it as a kind of epistemological test by constructing a stringent division between things and human minds. Although the projects are quite distinct, both of these artists located a disease of narration that, among other things, circulates within the construction of millen-nial thought.

One wants to be taken out of millennial thinking, to be transported. "Can't it, the utopian narrative, do something else?" is a question that one of Bloch's "erotic personalities" would ask. After all, such a "personality" might see herself lusting after the an-ticipatory terrain that seems to be foreclosed through the millennial narrative. The work of Breton might serve as a site, analogous perhaps to some local archi-tecture, that such a personality might situate herself in relation to . . . someplace else, a city, Montreal.

Control and chaos. The millennial narrative seems entirely incommensurate with the blue sky above a building's ochre pediment, or the character in a novel, *Main Brides*, named Norma jean who can interpret the "novelist's" dream better than the novelist, or the round of light on the face, then the knee, of a cyclist who cycles toward another century: the twenty-first or the twentieth – they seem slightly mixed up. Aren't there any cars in this book? And what about the old-fashioned title? Ironically, it celebrates and eroticizes an eroded (im)"pediment."[2] This is the site in which Scott's female characters enlist their own libidinal energies to benefit themselves, however qualified (imperfect) the benefit might be. A millennial hopelessness is subverted by the novelist's courtship of pleasure and by a certain "transposition of aesthetic categories into actual experience" (Nicholls 279).

There is always more than one narrative, more than one possible outcome, and more than one possible impasse. If there is the splitting of men and women into class-designed reproductive functions,[3] there are other accounts in which women invent themselves with a certain tenacity in the face of prevalent dangers: the narrative of rape, violence, murder, control of the bodies of women can design the conditions for another form of narrative that entirely, and dangerously, ignores "victimage"; the stereotypical version of this goes something like, "It's not going to happen to me/us, I/we're not like other women." A challenge, then, is to put "victimage" in the right place – by constructing a record of the liberating practice of self-invention without ignoring the dangers women face generically. One might entertain the utopic emotion, the desire "to know the ecstasy of the body's energy when it is not repressed by partriarchal rules and interdictions" (Brossard 37). In *Main Brides*,

> She imagines them behind those sprouting orbs or swordpoints, rising from cornices and pediments in mock aggression towards the sky. . . It's true – the *mam-bo*-dancing woman stupidly spoiled pleasure on the trip to Cuba, by continually recalling she'd become (by proxy) an unfortunate statistic. Not that Lydia blames her. But she never focuses on statistics . . . She prefers another approach to History . . . She focuses on the music. Also keeping down (with a gesture of her hand) an inner voice saying: "things happen randomly to women no matter what they do." (98)

The connecting of those things that are typically kept separate such as erotic desire and rape, or aesthetic pleasures and statistics, with automatic/chance events is what brings Breton as a figure and a literary predecessor into Scott's novel in its beginning pages through the portrait of Nanette.[4] Scott's and Breton's writing practices can be associated through their exploratory uses of autobiography. Scott is at pains to make us aware in the very structure of her book of the autobiographical impulse in her novel writing; in so doing, she displaces and critiques various notions of autobiography in literature, especially as they relate to clichés about women novelists. Bringing Breton into the biographical realm of her novel is a claim for a direct affiliation with a modernist male writer. Such an open acknowledgment can serve as a rebuke to those who think either that women should only tell their own stories or that it is women who have the weakness of only telling their own stories – since Breton, himself, subverts conventional novelistic practice by using various forms of narrative, including autobiography, in his writing of *Nadja*.

Main Brides is structured on a series of written portraits of women, and the first portrait is of a young woman, Nanette, who resembles Nadja. Like Nadja, Nanette enters the narrative reading Breton's manifestoes. Like Nadja, Nanette has exotic dark circles under her eyes and her clothes are the object of much attention, "hair now attached in wings atop her head; vaguely Slavic eyes looking oriental with the additional strokes of makeup; face white as a mask; lips cherry red; black décolleté leotard under her leather jacket" (30). She has a youthful revolutionary spirit characterized by an interior radicality and overt intellectualism qualified by a sense of damage. The possibility of things going entirely wrong for Nanette are not as great as for Nadja, for Nanette is the product of another era and loves her mother. She possesses what might be thought of as "an intransitive mental feeling of being in love" (Bloch, *Principle of Hope* 70) and she is inspired by Breton – her version of Breton: believing in nothing but chance and starting out from her own apartment "to discover what chance could bring" (28).

In a sense, Nanette's agency is indicated by her innocent choice to identify with Breton while she is also identified with Nadja (to what degree, one might

ask, can one separate the character from the author?)
through the observations/portraiture of the narrator.
Nanette does not seem to make a distinction, really,
between the author Breton and the figure of Nadja –
one being the product of the other. Scott's novel
questions the degree to which its character, Nanette,
is well-served by her ability to play the parts of both
Breton and Nadja. Can a woman constructively occupy or embody the position of philosopher and
femme savante? Can she acquire the power of the
philosopher within the discourses of this dual situation? Fuck whom she wants? Tap into unconscious
resources of the imagination, court chance and survive? Does she, the hypothetically real young woman
represented by the fictional Nanette, have as good a
chance of surviving as André Breton, the man, did?

Behind the maskings, the portraiture, in Scott's
book are questions that exceed the limits of the novel.
We as readers are tempted into flirting with the
notion that Nanette is based on a real person in Scott's
life. Where does the real end and fiction begin? This
question is too simple! Unless one also applies it to
Breton. Scott's manipulation of the likeness between
Nanette and Nadja is a kind of trick, a trick to ask the
reader to question likenesses, the likenesses assigned
women and, therefore, also Breton's likeness i.e. representation of Nadja. Subtly *Main Brides* interrogates
the notion of transposing the aesthetic category (like
novel) into actual existence – if a woman is writing
the "novel" where would actual existence begin? If
she were writing the "real" story of Nadja it would

not be the same as Breton's version. Where would Nanette's romantic imitation of the Breton/Nadja dyad fit? The "realism," dimensionality, complexity of Nanette lies not in her imitation but in her difference from those she imitates. She likes her mother. She is not mad. She acts fearless, because she wants to avoid fearful feelings and to reassure those around her, even though she is not entirely safe. Like Nadja, she is not careful. Unlike Nadja, she reserves for herself and not those men she might fear even a little more than she does (she is enamoured of chance which brings with it, for a woman, danger) the philosophical position which placed Breton and Nadja in a profound power imbalance. Nanette's psychological victimage is related to physical power and separated from intellectual power. Yet her intellectual power and/or potential intellectual powers cannot be the only answer to the question: do the present and future Nanettes of the world have as good a chance of surviving as André Breton?

Lydia, the portraitist, is also identified with Breton. Lydia's attitude toward Nanette is both maternal and sexual just as Breton's relationship to Nadja is both paternal and sexual. Like Breton the author of *Nadja*, Scott the author of *Main Brides* implicates herself as consequent to her character – posed as a hypothetically "real" person. Scott directs the reader's attention to this self-implication by indicating a subtle similarity of invasive, voyeuristic desire between her narrator, Lydia, and Breton. Lydia stands transparently for the author: the author's lusts and intellectual passions, including utopian emotion and transgressive desire, are mediated through Lydia. In constructing a fiction that tilts into autobiography, Scott challenges the autobiography that tilts into fiction. Scott assumes a more careful position in regard to Nanette than Breton assumed with the "real" Nadja. This position of care is exemplified in her looking for "possibility" in the figure of Nanette – a future-leaning and unknown promise, the anticipatory utopian emotion. What Breton did, through his literary use of his relationship with Nadja, is foreclose on his own utopian vision: for he sought the proof of his own great ideas in another, in effect cancelling the openness of possibility that results in transformation for someone other than himself. Breton created a paradox and arrived at an impasse (remorse), with Nadja returned to her "prison" and Breton left with his "freedom."

The question of such complicity is no easy matter. The need to account for the emotional pain derived from the suffering of an other or others seems to be central to the motivation of both Breton's and Scott's works. Breton's remorse may be what decides that the book is written, and Scott's melancholic double, Lydia, forms her narrative, in part, around the difficulty of knowing that her own suffering and pleasures are the suffering and pleasures of other women. Also, in this sense, Breton and Scott visit the problem of the part and the whole through self-implication without either turning against the self or condemning the other, willing as each is to suffer, celebrate, and know the unanswerable aspects of agency and causality; therefore, with great subtlety, Scott aligns herself with Breton's culpability while orchestrating a critique of the problem of *Nadja*. In this light, one might think of the Nanette chapter of *Main Brides* as a response to Breton's opening lines of *Nadja*, "Whom do I haunt?"

The transportation of art into life ought to be questioned, not because the association of "the real" with the aesthetic is wrong, but because powerful (hidden) ideologies can go along for the ride. Breton's normative patriarchal ideology of gender is neither one and the same as his revolutionary poetics nor is it entirely separate. More than acknowledging Breton as a predecessor, Scott has made use of him as a figure, a ghostly figure, to examine questions about the relationship between the aesthetic and lived experience. Breton's ghostliness is in part due to the question not resting, not being put to rest in the book.

Women assume powerful positions in the world by making their own desires and designs present and central to their projects, thereby unlinking their desires and energies from patriarchal repression. Irrespective of the alignment I have suggested, Scott does not make André Breton central to her feminist novel. She invents: he haunts. He is a part, a ghost, a residue of her epoch, and she makes use of his project for her own purposes – that is, to refuse repression i.e. the repression of transgressive fantasies, voyeuristic pleasures, lesbian and heterosexual desires, and relationships to and appropriation of urban and public space, and to invest imaginatively in all of the above.

If another formulation of a contained community is the separation of feminine (object) from masculine (subject), Scott's novel contests this history (Lydia "prefers another approach to History" [98]) – the traditional masculinist attitudes toward women artists of the avant-garde – and assumes authority over an array of sophisticated strategies in relationship to language, textuality, polemical positioning, and the "uncanny." She also demonstrates the distance between the utopian desire of liberation and the real while positioning her very contemporary feminism to talk back to history without foreclosing the forward-looking, anticipatory possibilities of imaginative investments.

Thus we find Scott in public. The intellectual matter/s of the text exceed the tidiness of the story. Interiority is turned into the world and subverted by the world. And this world includes the carnivalesque ghost of André Breton. Through this figure, she links the novel to other literary and art projects that exceed any particular avant-garde history (the novel as installation, for instance), and contaminates fiction with her own literary biography. The portraitist is always implicated in the portraits: they are processual and they rely on chance and habitat. The location for the portraits is always in public, in a bar. The portraitist Lydia/Scott sits in the bar and extrapolates from what she knows of the women who come and go from the bar, inventing their "fictional" lives. The bar in which

Lydia the character sits is the same bar in which Scott writes her novel. The sense of the novel is that it is drawn from life *and* the life of the mind. This is the utopian trajectory of the book, for what is taken from life becomes the basis for an exploration of utopian emotion that does not know exactly what it is looking for. Not knowing how the portrait will turn out contributes to the over-all open-endedness of the book and also to its provocative ending.

Whereas Breton placed the aesthetic within the real, Scott relies on degrees of displacement between notions of the aesthetic and the real in the construction of *Main Brides*; thus, she engages similar questions about the aesthetic and the real but to different ends. One can see this very clearly in her use of "background." The act of inventing women who both reflect the creative processes and energies of women and represent an open-ended possibility occupies the foreground of the novel. The background is occupied by two things: a singular image (that of a dead body in a park – eventually revealed as the body of a young woman) and the affect of male violence against women.[5] In placing male violence in the background, Scott effectively separates the erotic imaginations and desires of women from violent acts. Rape and other acts of violence deform and inhibit the desires of the women characters of her book, and she portrays each of them as struggling to keep violence from intervening in their projections and projects – which include romantic adventuring, performance, running radio shows, entrepreneurship, and intellectual play.

The background omnipresence of violence is struggled against. It is difficult to hold it in mind. It is hard for the reader to hold it in mind as she is tricked into more optimistic versions of identification with the subjects. These women are all putting themselves together as fascinating and fascinated self-creations. They all seem to be part of a utopic construction: they precede their objects, and the urban environment is theirs to make of it what they will.

At the end of the book, the foreground and the background meet. A confrontation is devised. A man, who may have been stalking someone or no one all along, winds his way into the foreground of the narrative. Is he, is this one, really dangerous? It may be a matter of a judgement call. The woman in the radio station, working late at night, takes out her knife waiting for the male aggressor to appear. The novel enacts a kind of revenge against the fictional death of the young woman in the park – the displaced signifier of the young women murdered in a classroom in Montreal.

This woman is ready. She can defend herself, unlike the girl in the park, unlike the students. She has taken her own survival into account. But the novel also, if it is indeed engaging the struggle between utopian desire and violence, suggests that the struggle reaches a splitting point. Will all of our energies be subsumed in combat and our utopian emotion depleted? How far can we go? Before some version of a splitting millennial narrative takes its toll?

NOTES

1   This essay first appeared in Romana Huk, ed., *Assembling Alternatives* (Hanover, NH: Wesleyan UP-UPNE, 2002). Reprinted by permission.

2   Architecture in Scott's novel is erotically charged. On the one hand, the concept of the bride and the architectural ornament are artifacts of the past (and impediments to change); but on the other hand, in so far as they are dynamically interconnected in a process of decay and change, they register Scott's interpretation of Québécois *modernité*. This particular cultural *modernité* roughly lies between American Modernism and Post-modernism. The Québécois avant-garde does not separate the concept of modernism and post-modernism into competing terrains. Thus, traditional gender roles and architecture serve metaphorically as aspects of the structure of Scott's novel, which observes that the nineteenth-century (arcane) novel and the novel of the twenty-first century are coextensive.

3   Margaret Atwood's *The Handmaid's Tale* (1985) would fill the slot of this kind of millennial narrative.

4   A meta-textual connection involves Scott's invention of Nanette as derived from Breton's invention of *Nadja*: the lesbian writer takes over the project of the heterosexual author.

5   In her article "Writing from the Border," Barbara Godard discusses the murders in the context of Scott's novel (*Trois* 11.1-2 [1996]: 167-180).

WORKS CITED

Bartkowki, Frances. *Feminist Utopias*. Lincoln, NE: U of Nebraska P, 1989.

Bloch, Ernst. *The Principal of Hope*. Trans. Neville Plaice, Stephen Plaice and Paul Knight. Vol. 1. Cambridge: MIT Press, 1995.

Breton, André. *Manifestoes of Surrealism*. 1969. Trans. Richard Seaver and Helen R. Lane. Ann Arbor: U of Michigan P, 1993.

——. *Nadja*. Trans. Richard Howard. New York: Grove, 1960.

Brossard, Nicole. *The Aerial Letter*. Trans. Marlene Wildeman. Toronto: Women's Press, 1988.

Nicholls, Peter. *Modernisms*. Berkeley: U of California P, 1995.

Robbe-Grillet, Alain. *For a New Novel: Essays on Fiction*. Trans. Richard Howard. New York: Grove, 1982.

Scott, Gail. *Main Brides: Against Ochre Pediment and Aztec Sky*. Toronto: Coach House, 1993.

Writing from the Border: Gail Scott on "The Main"

> You write in the Chinese book (moving from back to front): *Dear — : Can one woman be every (any) thing to another? Is this real? Are we real?"*
>
> Gail Scott, *Main Brides* 126[1]

> Lydia thinks: "I'm confusing art with real. I'll have to unwind the thread – ." But she feels resentful. Maybe at the trompe l'oeil effect in everything they did."
>
> Gail Scott, *Main Brides* 206

These fragments function as "graffiti indicating the small solidarities" (*Main Brides* 16), unwinding a thread for me through Gail Scott's portrait gallery of women facing the end of the millennium, oscillating between apocalypse and nostalgia, waiting "[n]ot for love . . . but for History. For the greedy decade to give way to lust and revolution" (32) while trying to "get the 19th century and 20th century together before the 21st arrives" (48). Waiting is the main "action" in a book where seemingly "not much happens in terms of plot" (Persky). Sitting in a Portuguese café on The Main, where she shifts between wine and coffee with an altered consciousness blurred between the numbness of forgetting and the elation of fanta-

sizing, the narrator, Lydia, "finds such delays infinitely aesthetic. Waiting also opens up the space of
melancholy which she sometimes cultivates in revolt
against certain positivist ideas" (*Main Brides* 33).
Among these ideas are questions of the symbolic, of
narrative, of fact, that is, of history. Lydia longs for
"brides," images of women of the future, who will
connect art and life to make a new history based not
on violence but on aesthetic detail. Written in the
present participle of becoming, this is a different kind
of history, one of process, a "fluid thing . . . full of
nuance, broad, accessible, instead of mean and categorical" that will accord women "the same (material)
capacity for existence" (199) and image them into the
trajectory of the human species, sculpt them in bas-
relief as pediments on the mansarded roofs in the
heart of Montreal and, apotheosized against the blue
sky, lift them out of fear. Formulated in the title of
the connecting interludes as "the sky is all I want" is
Lydia's desire for boundlessness.

Gail Scott, like Lydia, reflects upon the inter-
twined issues of spatiality, temporality and desire
from her border position between centuries, between
cultures. Among the most prominent of contemporary anglo-Quebec writers, Scott has meditated on the
political implications of writing in English in Quebec
as a woman, of the problematics of textuality and
subjectivity within the complex relations of language
and identity this borderline situation of enunciation
entails, as these inform a tactics for constituting the
"real." On "the uncanny edge of language" is how

Scott frames her position, one of the *unheimlich* as in-between (*Spaces Like Stairs* 62). Rather than "destruction," this offers "wonderful expansion," as Hélène Cixous sees it:

> questioning (in) the between (letting oneself be questioned) of same *and of* other . . . ; undoing death's work by willing the togetherness of one-another, infinitely charged with a ceaseless exchange of one with another . . . beginning again only from what is most distant, from self, from other, from the other within. A course that multiplies transformations by the thousands. (86)

Linda Leith, in turn, considers Scott's first "novel" *Heroine* in its "emblems of marginality" as exemplary of contemporary English fiction in Quebec perched "on the social and literary periphery" of the Canadian literary institution ("Quebec Fiction" 101). Acknowledging the great importance of being a "minority anglophone in a French milieu," Scott comments on this "becoming-minor" (Deleuze and Guattari) as a process of disidentification:

> I think it taught me more about my own culture than the francophone culture, because I learned to see it – my own culture – through the other person's eyes, with all its crazy permutations – including its role of political oppressor . . . a vision that comes from standing on the outside looking in. ("On the edge of change" 17, 19)

Contradictions abound: solidarity with Quebecois national affirmation produces a "diminished self-image" which sets Scott at odds with the "positive upbeat" image expected of feminist writers in English (*Spaces Like Stairs* 63).

Scott's orientation is different from most English-language writers in Quebec: she turns not to a recollected Ontario, like Hugh Hood in the *The New Age* series; nor to the constitution of the apparatuses of a distinctive anglo-Quebec literary institution like the "Quanglos," writers focused around the periodical *Matrix* or Q-Spell (Linda Leith, Kenneth Radu, David Solway, etc.) to compensate for the perceived lack of "institutional supports (not only local English-language publishers of fiction, but magazines, literary awards, informed criticism, good press coverage, etc.)" (Leith, "Quebec Fiction" 99); nor (except to explode it) to the prevalent mode of "genre fiction" – sci fi and crime fiction especially (102) – like George Szanto, David Homel or Edward Phillips; nor to historicizing fossilizations *on* francophone culture, typical of nineteenth-century writers such as Rosanna Leprohon and D.C. Scott.

On the contrary, Scott has aligned herself with French-speaking Quebec writers, participating in such publishing ventures as *Spirale*, a cultural periodical, but most extensively with a group of feminist writers with whom she collectively published a record of their discussions on language and gender, *La théorie, un dimanche*. While her journalism was produced in English-language media, her first "literary" texts were published in French. Writing *out of* French-language literary codes *on* Quebecers *toward* an English-speaking reader, Scott has been "excited" rather than "threatened" "by the things happening here in Quebec in the last 15 years" ("Interview," *Matrix* 24), a period in which "the space between politics and art closed somewhat with the decolonization movement" and in which "feminism" actively worked the "conjuncture" of "formalist" and of "highly politicized" work on language and genre (Scott, "On the Edge" 18). As she elaborates, "Québécois women have found a place from which to write that's somewhere between speech and writing . . . Language is a voice that has more texture than just the content of what it's saying" ("Interview," *Matrix* 24). What Scott invokes here is the impact in Quebec of a concept of language as *délire* (or nonsense) which has become the central tenet of a French philosophical tradition that emphatically rejects a theory of language as an instrument of communication wielded with mastery for a theory of language as a process through which the subject is constituted in an experience of possession. *Délire*, a mode of metalinguistic discourse, implies a practice of language close to theory (Lecercle 155). Language carries a story of the passions of the individual body: the letter, a paradoxical element, constitutes erogenous zones in a process of inscription, turning a human body into a particular subject. The body appears on the surface as an abstraction, the mark for an absent object. In the inability to master these signs by abstracting letters from bodies, the subject falls prey to a disorderly multitude of signs or *délire*. Desire is produced by the illusion of a

missing primary object marked by a letter (Lecercle
147-149). The relations between language and body
may be those of "designation," "signification," or
"device" through which the body's screams come to
the surface as words (39). Against a view of writing
as rational control with the valorization of syntax is
another of writing as risk-taking, as experiment with
a device which is a personal solution to pain and
suffering, ruffling smoother syntactic links with its
particular rhythmic pulse. Beyond a chain of imita-
tions in the realm of common sense lies the excess of
an idiolect or intensive use of language, the trajectory
of a desiring subject in surfaces of sense.

Scott has been preoccupied with such texture of
language and form. Writing between languages has
obliged her to invent her very medium, to engage in
"language-centred" work on signs as affective and
effective relays rather than as cognitive representations and so to make English vibrate differently
with (Latin) rhythms from Quebec. Such bilingual
confluency introduces a contradictory dynamic ("Interview," *Paragraph* 4), worked through in her particular device of the parenthesis as a paradoxical
element that performatively engages the zigzag movement of narrative semiosis, where signifying surfaces
overlap and bounce off each other in a movement of
proliferation and dispersion, rather than one of
centring and integration. Fictional events occur at the
level of discourse in such movements of accidental
assemblage.

Differences in theory, in texture, in register, become sites of strained encounters in *Main Brides* when, thinking more in English with her lover from Alberta, the "Canadian girl" "loses the capacity for immediate abstraction that comes with speaking French" (*Main Brides* 123). Such differences, moreover, inform divergent understandings of the political, as demonstrated in the dialogues of the deaf staged between Quebec and Ontario. Z. has, through effort, achieved a "perfect surface" (153). Lydia develops an obsession for reading bodies as a politics of desire: "Entering a spell. Until all she sees is the exterior of things. Exterior equals real. . . . [A] woman observing various layers of society (from her place in the bar)" (99). Lydia is described as "one of those people you meet travelling who feels better in another language" spending hours in her room dressing up "to pass" (53). As the narrative function of focalization, Lydia is nothing but a textual surface, a series of projections, negations, displacements of signs, a constant troping. Lydia *insists* in an activity of (re)reading the corporeal surfaces of women, her identity returned to her from the site of the Other, in the gaze ("you") of her seven "brides." However, this focus on the fashion and architecture of subcultures, on textual surfaces of meaning, is challenged as apolitical by Norma jean from Ontario: "Ouiiii, la mohde, maiy. . . . Sure style's everything in art. But don't you think it's important to somehow represent social notions, like race, class?" "Ou bien," the woman replied, provocatively, "comme l'indépendance du Québec?" (193).

The debate over the politics of language and form is more frequently resolved differently. Scott stages the process of disidentification by bringing into her work the externalized voice of an anglo-Canadian feminist critic by way of staging the contradiction of her fixating on the culture of the loved and hated other.

> "Your work isn't positive enough to be feminist," says a feminist writer from English Canada. "It doesn't show an upbeat enough image of solidarity." "But," I reply, at first feebly, then angrily, "It's about the relationship between thinking and feeling; about the struggle between her feminist consciousness – in both its greatness and its limitations – and social constructs, memory, dreams, nightmares." (*Spaces Like Stairs* 131)

The problem Scott's work stages is that of an audience, of a discursive community, the problem of address or enunciation. Where can she locate the "you" through which to engage in the dialogue of writing that would constitute her as "I," as subject and author? How can "I" participate in the *polis*, the city, the community constituted by "we"? Scott specifically critiques identity politics with their epistemic/ontological regime based in a fixed concept of self, what she characterizes as "withdrawal into a kind of egotism. I.e. . . . a strong identifying narrative" (*Main Brides* 162), in favour of a notion of identity as a moving site of signifying effects constituted intra(er)textually: "Lydia (*the portrait*)" is a subject-effect produced through reading (197; emphasis added). In this, Scott comes to *la cité* as "a feminist at the carnival" (*Spaces Like Stairs*) to transgress the limits not only of patriarchy, but also of anglo-Canadian women's writing where the feminist revolution is centred on content and representation rather than on language as signifying praxis. This dilemma of the interlocutor is framed compellingly by the situation of the narrator, Lydia, sitting alone at a table in the bar, gazing at the women passing by and inventing imaginary dialogues with/for them, trying to constitute a community and herself as subject within it. As Scott explains to a Toronto interviewer,

> writing is about constructing a subject – this is the point at which writing and life are so intertwined. [I'm constantly thinking of new ways that a person could be that would be ecologically harmonious, non-oppressive, and non-racist and non-oppressed as well, not putting up with any bullshit.] When I write, I address other people with whom I've been discussing these issues. That *rapport* is really important. (Scott, "On the Edge" 19)

"Technologies of gender" (and of nation, we could add) are how Teresa de Lauretis terms such protocols and modes of address (speech genres), modalizations for configuring the real that distinguish, within language, between subject and object, between insider and outsider, and constitute an imagined community through the exchange of signs. ("Teresa of Santa Cruz," it should be noted, has a walk-on role in *Main Brides*.) Empty terms or shifters, "you" and "I" constitute subjectivity relationally (and hierarchically) within the discursive positions socially available. At the site of enunciation, by positing "you" as addressee, at a point of temporal and spatial disjunction (then, there) from the moment of speaking, "I" constitute myself as subject across this gap. "You" from this position of subject of *énoncé* reciprocally constitute "me" as "you" – subject of the statement. Within an "ordinary" or "extensive" or "reterritorializing" function of language as representation, these deictic relations are characterized by distinction and complementarity between speaking and spoken subject (Deleuze and Guattari 20). In situations of asymmetry or power differential, "the message doesn't refer back to an enunciating subject who would be its cause, no more than to a subject of the statement (*sujet d'énoncé*) who would be its effect" (18). The slippage and gap between the conditions under which the text is enunciated (message of the enunciating subject) and the denotated content of its message (subject of the *énoncé*) disrupt the myth of a single fixed meaning in a movement of "deterritorialization" and heteroglossia, characterized by an "intensive" or "asignifying" usage of language in which there is a disjunction between a text's performative and referential fields (19). These disjunctions introduce a functional change in sign system or semiosis that produces different contiguities, different potentialities for combination, through which the relations and meanings between signifiers are modified.

Such a movement constitutes the discursive displacement of "becoming-minor" (27) which, for Deleuze and Guattari in *Kafka: Toward a Minor Literature*, signifies an accelerating rhythm of dispersion and proliferation to produce "metamorphosis" and variation rather than "metaphor" or "resemblance" (22). Marking a language for "strange and minor uses" (17), such "deterritorialization" is the condition of "minor literature," characterized by its paradoxical (im)possibility – "the impossibility of *not* writing, because national consciousness, uncertain or oppressed, necessarily exists by means of literature," the impossibility of writing *in* the "national" language because of the irreducible difference from it (16). Nonetheless, this site of disjunctive synthesis produces an "active solidarity" where every "individual intrigue" is "contaminated by the political domain" and constitutes a *collective* subject-position (16-17). Writing is figured in terms of (self-)marginalization or of boundary crossing, rather than of origin or distinction. Writing from a site of dislocation or disjunction of signification entails experimentation, writing as research into the as yet unthought. The productive force of proliferating connections along a line of variation instituted by the multiple possibilities for combination on the metonymic chain which exceed a language of mastery or transcendent-dominated reality on the metaphoric axis is the logic of the series or problematic set in motion by the aleatory point or question, the "throw of the dice" (Deleuze). Chance generates narrative in *Main Brides*, whether in the form of the surrealist games of Nanette whom the narrator informs us "deserves another chance" (*Main Brides* 62) or in the things that happen "randomly to women no matter what they do" (98) which the fiction works through repetition both to repress and to express.

It is this logic of the "and and and" (Deleuze 16) that I want to pursue in my reading of *Main Brides,* locating its politics of address in its work on narration as fragment, as series, and on the complex relation between narrator and character in the process of mutual constitution/dissolution. Along the lines of Mikhail Bakhtin's consideration of relations between author and hero in terms of exotopy, this invites reflection on ethical and addressive answerability when truth can be only a horizon. Such a valorization of outsidedness or alterity produces a layering or blurring, the logic of a thin or permeable border, for it rests upon a distinction between "inside" and "outside," a logic by which blurring of others sharpens the view of self; on the other hand, such a blurring allows for a parallax view that undermines the absolute authority of any monocular (monologic) perspective and offers to feminists a space of differentiation in the interstice with transformative potential. In opposition to the single "point de capiton" proposed by Lacan, the "multiple capture" or disjunctive synthesis of this logic of the "and" does not reunite but stutters, as trace of a frayed line that breaks off in connecting, "a sort of line of flight, active and creative" (Deleuze 16). Scott marks this interstice, this break-out, with the parenthesis. The logic of outside in/inside out or

the logic of the moebius strip has been framed by Scott
in terms of political parallax as border crossing to a
home ground become foreign territory – "A *Visit* to
Canada" (*Spaces Like Stairs*; emphasis added). This
text opens with a scene of reading where English-Canadian poet, Erin Mouré from Calgary, reads a translation of a Greek poet to Scott in a café on The Main,
Montreal's moveable site of the in-between, between
French and English, space of (im)migration, space of
phantasmatic figurations of identity. The recursive
reach of mirrors within mirrors in the café is a figure
for "the words revealing the possible richness in the
reading/writing relationship of a work that crosses
cultures, sexual boundaries . . ." (*Spaces Like Stairs*
45). These crossings are, nonetheless, inevitably
traces of the different as same – the indifference of
bicultural and/or sexual difference. This is the "other
of the same," rather than the "other of the other"
(Irigaray):

> [I]n such transmissions, there is terrible loss. Particu-
> larly when the reader/writer stand in a conflictual re-
> lationship to each other. In Canada, for example, the
> strikingly different Québécois and Canadian percep-
> tions (readings) of the October Crisis are part of two
> ongoing different narratives in what is officially a
> common history . . . Clearly they are more than con-
> tent, *a question of texture.* Even an anglophone living
> in Québec, provided she lives a good part of the time
> in French, starts to feel this difference in her body af-
> ter awhile. At least, she starts to feel it on visits to the
> other culture: English Canada. (*Spaces Like Stairs* 45;
> emphasis added)

As Scott points out in her framing comments to
"Spaces Like Stairs," "the question of self and other,
of differences and likenesses among women . . . has
become more complex in this decade" (44). Questions of nationality, ethnicity, race, class and sexual
orientation have come to trouble any stable notion of
identity. While "the mutual respect between feminists
from Québec and Canada" has done much to "raise
consciousness" of these issues of complex identification, nonetheless vestiges of power relations remain:

> Even as an English Quebecer who has absorbed con-
> siderable influences from a French-language culture
> not the Same as the dominant English culture of other
> provinces, I have occasionally felt a small personal
> malaise regarding this lack of space in Canada for the
> hearing of difference . . . But the experience has been
> part of my learning how not hearing the other closes
> space for each of us (both speaker and addressee).
> (*Spaces Like Stairs* 44)

This problematic of representation as rhetorical violence is broached when Scott remarks on her inability
"to articulate a bridge" among differences: relations
among cultures and races are characterized more by
abysses (Scott, "Introduction: Women of Letters"
18). The metaphor of the bridge, as Kathy Mezei has
written, has long been the dominant trope for translation in the Canadas, which has been carried out
under the humanist imperative to "know thyself"
through the Other (Simon). Marked by the structures

of the dialectic, this carrying across became a movement of incorporation in which difference was absorbed into the selfsame at a higher level of synthesis. Scott leaves the bridge for the contact zone in between, site of charged encounters and superpositions. In *Main Brides*, the binary of French/English or east/west is displaced by The Main, site of multiple cultural crossings. The Portuguese café instigates a Latin beat for other riffs or encounters on a north/south axis. As boundary where one thing becomes another, the café on The Main is not so much a site for marking distinctions as for facilitating overlaps, contradictions, paradoxes. From her seat at the window overlooking the street, Lydia notes the instability of signs of identity in the work of the sign-shop men. "But no matter what the angle, the French-only version fails to cover the larger English-Hebrew-Arabic scripts showing underneath" (*Main Brides* 155).

In recent years, Gail Scott has been one of the most lucid and ironic observers of such cross-cultural engineering projects. The edginess of her prose manifests itself in the sarcasm of the title "Donkey Riding," a section focused on Norma jean, a Marilyn Monroe throwback from the Ontario of the 1950s, whose stereotypical view of Quebec is figured in the refrain Lydia hums repeatedly: "Were you ever in Québec / Stowing timber on a deck / Donkey riding, donkey riding" (175). Figuration of the "hegemonizing standard" of Toronto, now restricted to young campers, this song used to be sung by sailors "loading the riches of Québec on the decks of British ships. Something about the king with the golden crown coming to take the lumber" (172). What was once a chant of political resistance has now been appropriated by the powerful elite as a rhyme for excluding through ridicule. At this point, the asymmetry of power differentials interrupts Lydia's line of seven Canadian beauties. Scott's image of the reading in the café of recursive mirrors, refracting and dispersing the self to infinity, encapsulates her awareness of the fragility of these projects of responsibility to the other, of their tentativeness, of the force of the gap and the contamination of the overlap within the current order of English-French relations (147).

Such a logic of blurring with its overflowing of boundaries is staged in Lydia's "altered consciousness" and her obsessive relations with others in the café who become variously, simultaneously, projections and/or introjections of her phantasmatic identifications. Lydia as framing narrator reaches out towards the character or "she," and towards the reader or "you," (figuring "herself" in both these positions as well as "I") incrementally bridging the gaps between anecdotes with images that function as relays. The "woman dressed like a mandarin" of Lydia's frame (136) merges with the performance artist "dressed as a kind of mandarin" in the section "Z. Who Lives over the Sign Shop" (140), while the colour of her suit jacket picks up the red of the officer's tunic from "Main Bride Remembers Halifax," and the red A-line coat of Norma jean in "Donkey Riding." Also, the "AIEEEEEEEEEEEEEEEEEE"

(94) of "you," the narrator of "Dis-May," resonates
in the opening phrase of Lydia's interlude a page
later: "What if she screamed out loud?" (96), so
making accidental connections between "narrator"
and "character" through writing that will articulate
the "real."

> what's real?
> the problem is   in the space
> . . .
> after ten years of textual trying are we ready to say
>   how to say
> what   (our) real is?
>
> *(Spaces Like Stairs* 107)

These lines from the title essay *Spaces Like Stairs*, are
framed by a meditation on the "end of genre" or
contemporary strategies for writing which are at the
"crossroads" of several discourses and are the work
of a mind "without those distinctions between real-
ity/theory/fiction." This is a space of the in-between,
of the gap or excess of signification, a "pregnant
pause" – "(in this space was born the sentence)" (107)
– of the parenthesis, a textual feature which is a major
technology in *Spaces Like Stairs* and, more recently,
in *Main Brides*. Parenthesis is a rhetorical device for
circumventing the barriers between levels of language, for crossing the frontiers between different
fields of discourse. A structure allowing multiple or
irrelevant groupings to emerge by inviting readers to
cut up utterances into contradictory fragments, it
produces syntactic ambiguity whereby language de-

stroys its own system of representation, metaphor. The rules of segmentation are forced here, introducing impossible or illegitimate combinations by way of metonymic accretion. Parentheses speak to the ongoing struggle of enunciation, to disjunction rather than complementarity, in the narrator's diminished sense of self as she attempts to write within the parameters of the dominant symbolic, and to the incompletion of her articulation of another frame for her written/writing self. This dislocation, which sends things spiralling in every direction, rather than forward in a single logical causal construction, privileges the metalinguistic properties of discourse. Such framebreaking scrutinizes the process of framing. Scott's concern is not with "writing a novel about X" but with the "process of writing" that will bring X into existence (*Spaces Like Stairs* 81), with writing that makes writing. The novel is not about the development of character through incident and plot, but rather about the importance of character and narrating-in-process, with a flow of words unleashing pathos, affect. Foundering rather than founding, it works not to consolidate a subject, but a singularity or arrangement, that is, a temporary and unstable collocation of desire. Here the blurred perspective and progressive dissolution of a narrative centre in the palimpsestic and paratactic forms produced by the parenthesis interrogate the "real" in a speculative fiction.

The "real," for Lacan, is the "impossible," that which "always comes back to the same place" in an uncanny return whose meaning continues to elude

GAIL SCOTT   135

the subject who lives in its grip without control over
or knowledge of it (Freud's repetition-compulsion or
death instinct) (Lacan 42). "Reality" is constructed by
a subject in the work of symbolic and imaginary
processes as a fiction that is a substitute for a lost
primary truth or trauma that is alone "real." "What's
real?" is a question that Scott, following Brossard,
frames instead as "Whose real?" to foreground the
instance of enunciation wherein are fixed the "effects
of the real" within a specific gendered ordering. In
this process of semiosis, signs are variously taken for
the "real" or as "fiction" depending on the manner in
which they are conceptualized, by whom and in
whose interests (Threadgold 2-3). Currently, there is
only a single practice and representation of the sexual: "the feminine occurs only within models and
laws devised by male subjects" (Irigaray 86). Woman
is limited to the maternal function under this Oedipal
contract, to marriage (integration) or death (exclu-
sion) within the triangular family romance it instan-
tiates. The impossibility of an identification "with the
sacrificial logic of separation and syntactical sequence
at the foundation of language and the social code" is
leading feminists to a rejection of a symbolic that has
constituted them as lack, as body on the side of
reproduction (Kristeva 199). Rejecting the subjective
limitations imposed upon them by such a position and
inserting themselves into history (195), feminists'
revolt against the symbolic order may produce
"deadly violence" or "cultural innovation" or both
(200). This has worked to increase the "complexity"

of women's identifications: significant in the challenge to this fictional economy is desire that would figure relations of exchange among women outside the paternal signifier.

"Intercepting the Real" to realign the boundaries between fiction and reality is crucial to the realization of the "aerial letter" (Brossard), that is, to the actualization of becoming-women through the project of making women's words fly beyond sanctioned order. This feminist project of "jam[ming] sociality" (Cixous 96) is a discursive combat waged through fiction. Writing is a tool which permits reflection on the modalities of ordering thought, this work on the perception of the virtual/real taking place in fiction that works upon reality to its loss (Brossard 23). Discourses of the "unreal" are deployed in a strategic and self-reflexive manner to "make visible" the sexist discourses coding the distinctions between fiction and reality, as well as between genres (fiction/theory, short-story/novel, novel/prose-poem), contradictions lodged within textuality in a sexual politics of genre. Blurring the traditional boundaries – formal and ideological – between fiction and reality, such strategic fictions work to expose the discursive constraints of the masculine imaginary and to offer a critical position in excess of these limits. Scott's speculative fiction interrogates the operation of discourse and textuality in the mediation of the real, exposing the literary as the articulation of identificatory fictions that legitimate certain (patriarchal) truth-claims and disallow others. Significantly, this fiction is framed in terms similar to those of Brossard's project of producing "aerial women": the seven "brides" silhouetted against the Montreal sky would actualize (Lydia's) boundless desire.

The space between genres is only one of the spaces Scott works with. This space of repetition and critique, both *heimlich* and *unheimlich* as Scott elaborates in "Spaces Like Stairs," this in-between of the text, of signification, of consciousness; this space of the middle voice, both subject and object, neither subject nor object, is a space where the subject acts upon itself. It is with such spaces that Scott ruses in her fiction theory, attempting to articulate strategies of the real, of boundary play as surface effects that will trace attempts at passage, movements of *sortie*, of desire embracing a succession of part objects, of the fragment reframed in the series. As she self-reflexively articulates in *Main Brides*,

> Lydia (having trouble focusing) returns to her portrait: anecdotal fragments organized – but not too rigorously – with a little space around them to open possibilities. Like Aztec art in the sense that their figures, carved on parapets, seemed projected towards the endless blue. Of course, under this dreamlike surface, lay darker, more insidious narratives promising ultimate disaster. Requiring more and more sacrifices in hopes of reprieve. (166-167)

Elsewhere, it is "statistics" that constitute the menace Lydia hopes to avoid with "some other kind of History. Compromising dream (multiple intuitions, possibilities) plus reality. Like the 13 Aztec heavens – all stacked up and graded in many different colours from dark earth to sky" (98). Whether as interval or as layering, an Aztec symbology offers possibilities for ordering that would escape History's "homocidal" propensities where sameness has a killing effect (135). Narrative for Lydia holds out the promise of the manageability of unspeakable loss which accompanies this passage, with the displacement of the referent and the multiplication of signifiers at the site of the lost referent.

Scott's work draws attention to this narrative function through its focus on the conflict between desire and the law of the father. It shows, by way of contrast through its lack of totality and coherency or mastery, the extent to which narrative strains for the effect of having filled in all the gaps. History, in the wake of Hegel, entails the establishment of causal chains and the discovery of origins. An alternative, genealogy, according to Nietszche, elaborates the circular tension between constitutive rules and that which constitutes the rules, for instance between romance and the Oedipal contract. Scott's work on boundary play follows yet another tactic focusing on the differential element or paradox, the relation between language and the human body – how sounds articulate meaning, how events caught in language are inseparable from the proposition in which they are expressed (Lecercle 95) – and the way the surface is both linking and separating. Mapping relations of inside and outside a system, frontiers can be denied, in which case the system collapses, or is forgotten and tamed, in a pedagogic fiction. Semiotic processes of disjunction operate at the border between two sets of elements or series, each of which is not the other, but whose addition does not form a totality (Lecercle 73) in an overlap of negation and connection or condensation and displacement.

Making use of "spaces like stairs" to connect a chain of part objects and gaps in a disjunctive series as desire zigzags, Scott works in the open weave of text, in the middle ground. Textually, this has been framed as the work of the aside, the parenthetical remark, through which a process of modulation is instituted whereby the relations between "I"and "you" are multiply articulated as the narrative centre, Lydia, dissolves into her seven "brides." Where there is not one but seven points of entry, narrative spirals in many different directions. Incompletion, gaps, digressions, parentheses, versions – so many strategies point to an awareness that there are still other meanings beyond what has been included. A narrative structured as holes and patches allows irrelevant or multiple groupings to emerge. The proliferation of structures points to where language as calculus fails and the desire of a subject emerges. Compulsive repetition functions as an attempt to encounter the "real." Paradoxically, an encounter with the "real" in a moment of insight or traumatic experience undoes the constructions of "reality" in a *délire* of repetition. Repetition orders ambiguous movements of reconstruction and disruption. In the impossibility of grasping "*a*" meaning, language, fiction, proliferate.

NOTES

1   This essay was originally published in a slightly different
     version in *Trois* 11.1-2 (1996): 169-180.

WORKS CITED

Brossard, Nicole. *The Aerial Letter*. Trans. Marlene Wildman.
     Toronto: Women's Press, 1988.

Cixous, Hélène, and Catherine Clément. *The Newly Born Woman*.
     Trans. Betsy Wing. Minneapolis: Minnesota UP, 1986.

Deleuze, Gilles. *Logique du sens*. Paris: Minuit, 1969.

Deleuze, Gilles, and Félix Guattari. *Kafka: Toward a Minor Lit-
     erature*. Trans. Dana Polan. Minneapolis: U Minnesota P,
     1985.

Irigaray, Luce. *This Sex Which Is Not One*. Trans. Carolyn Porter.
     Ithaca: Cornell UP, 1985.

Kristeva, Julia. *The Kristeva Reader*. Ed. Toril Moi. Oxford: Basil
     Blackwell, 1986.

Lacan, Jacques. *The Four Fundamental Concepts of Psychoanaly-
     sis*. Ed. Jacques-Alain Miller. Trans. Alan Sheridan. New
     York: Norton, 1978.

Lecercle, Jean-Jacques. *Philosophy Through the Looking Glass*.
     London: Hutchinson, 1985.

Leith, Linda. "Quebec Fiction in English During the 1980s: A Case
     Study in Marginality." *Quebec Studies* 9 (Fall 1989): 95-110.

Mezei, Kathy. "A Bridge of Sorts: The Translation of Quebec
     Literature into English." *Anglo-American Literary Relations*.
     The Yearbook of English Studies 15 (1985): 202-226.

Persky, Stan. "Scenes from a Montreal Café." *Globe and Mail* 3
     July 1993: C13.

Polytechnique, 6 décembre. Montreal: Remue-ménage, 1990.

Scott, Gail. "Author Replies." Reply to letter of Stan Persky. *Globe
     and Mail* 21 Aug. 1993: D7.

——— . "Interview with Gail Scott." By Beverley Daurio. *Paragraph*
     15.2 (Fall 1993): 3-7.

——— . "Interview with Gail Scott." By Linda Leith. *Matrix* 28
     (Spring 1989): 23-24.

———. *Main Brides*. Toronto: Coach House, 1993.

——. "On the edge of change." Interview with Barbara Carey. *Books in Canada* (Aug.-Sept. 1989): 15-19.

——. *Spaces Like Stairs*. Toronto: Women's Press, 1989.

Scott, Gail, et al. "Introduction: Women of Letters." Ed. Barbara Godard. *Collaboration in the Feminine: Writings on Women and Culture from* Tessera. Toronto: Second Story-Sumach, 1994. 9-19.

Scott, Gail, Louky Bersianik, Nicole Brossard, Louise Cotnoir, Louise Dupré, and France Théoret. *La théorie, un dimanche*. Montreal: Remue-ménage, 1988.

Simon, Sherry. "Volontés de savoir: Les préfaces aux traductions canadiennes." *Prefaces and Literary Manifestoes / Préfaces et manifestes littéraires*. Ed. E.D. Blodgett and A.G. Purdy. Edmonton: U of Alberta-RICL, 1990. 98-110.

Threadgold, Terry. *Feminine/Masculine and Representation*. Ed. Anne Cranny-Francis. Sydney: Allen & Unwin, 1990.

The Paris Arcades, the Ponte Vecchio and the Comma of Translation

SHERRY SIMON

Gail Scott's latest novel, *My Paris*, contains a device which she calls "the comma of translation."[1] This comma is something of an intruder in a book which is "imbued with the ghost of Gertrude Stein" (163) and with her opinions on language. Gertrude Stein banished the comma from modernist writing and, indeed, *My Paris* is written in a rigorously crafted modernist style, made up of sentence fragments separated by periods.[2] But Scott does use a few commas. These occur when the narrator uses a French expression which is followed by its translation. For instance, "mal foutue, badly shoed" (18) or the lyrics of a song, "Nous sommes les animaux," "we are animals" (72). About a third of the way into the novel, the narrator seems to provide an explanation. Evoking Stein's dictum against commas, she wonders, "But if comma of translation disappearing. What of French-speaking America remaining" (49).

Scott's comma of translation draws us into a rich web of thinking about language and translation which leads us from Paris to Montreal, from Gertrude Stein and Walter Benjamin to experimental writing in Quebec, from the modernist experience of expatriation to the postmodern reality of cultural hybridity. By posting signs of cultural difference, Scott is revising the modernist illusion of a nude and value-free formalism, its desire for universality. By placing translation within her novel, Scott is pointing towards a space which holds increasing significance in the contemporary world: the space where multiple languages gather, where translation and writing express the same impulse to use language contact creatively.

I would like to explore some of the connections created by the "comma of translation," connections that draw translation and writing together. At the same time, I would like to emphasize a shift in the mandate which Canadian translation seems to be giving itself. When Philip Stratford in the 1970s called translations of Quebec literature "news from the front," he was referring to an intense flurry of exchange between Quebec and English-Canadian literature, an exchange motivated by curiosity and fascination. Translators were called upon to "transmit" Quebec literary news to new readers. The informative and ambassadorial role, I would argue, is now being augmented by another dimension. Rather than acting exclusively as mediators, writer/translators are increasingly involved in creating hybrid literary texts which are informed by a double culture. The novels of Gail Scott, a writer/translator who expresses the tensions of a multilingual Montreal, are examples of such texts. Like other anglophones who write out of the dissonances and marginalities of their situation, Scott uses languages to link traditions, making her texts a crossroads of sensibilities.

The Arcades of Paris

The many allusions in *My Paris* to Gertrude Stein – and also to Walter Benjamin – remind us that Paris at the turn of the century was the capital of modernism and a cosmopolitan centre for expatriate writers and artists. For many, if not all of the English-language writers who lived in Paris, the experience of expatriation itself was at the heart of modernist rethinking of literary norms. "Translation" stands for a whole array of practices through which modernists used other languages and traditions for aesthetic innovation. These crossovers were not always made visible, however. The exceptional cases were the deviant and eccentric forms of trans-lingual writing conceived by Pound, Beckett and Joyce. For most of the other writers, however, translation was much more of an implicit practice, in the sense, for instance, in which it was said that Mina Loy "transferred futuristic theories to America," "translating" into English the aesthetics of Apollinaire and Marinetti (Burke 5).

Scott chooses to repair this omission, to restore visibility to translation by defying Stein's prohibition against commas and by placing the French language within her text. While *My Paris* is a work which renders homage to the audacity of modernism, and to the complexity of Gertrude Stein's rethinking of language, the novel at the same time takes its distance from some of Stein's practices and assumptions. In particular, Scott draws attention to cultural difference, critiquing Stein's position in the modernist negotiation of literary identities, giving visibility to the French language, making explicit and present the language through which Stein designed and re-thought her poetics.

But there is a second mythical presence in *My Paris* which intensifies the significance of translation in the novel. This presence is Walter Benjamin, whose *Passagen-Werk* (the Arcades Project) appears as a recurrent reference. This huge and unfinished project by Benjamin is a vast collection of notes on nineteenth-century industrial culture as it took place in Paris. Benjamin's experience of Paris, we recall, is strongly coloured by the spirit of Baudelaire, whose work, *Tableaux parisiens*, Benjamin himself translated into German. The preface to that translation, entitled "The Task of the Translator," has become a signal essay on translation, a dense and ambiguous text, which has lent itself to innumerable interpretations and commentaries.

The "comma of translation" leads us directly to Benjamin's reinterpretation of the role of translation. Benjamin's essay is notoriously hermetic,[3] but one of Benjamin's main arguments can perhaps be summarized as follows. Benjamin suggests that translation is less about transmitting a message than it is about revealing differences. The task of the translator, he suggests, is not to neutralize the difference between the original and the translation through the replacement of one with the other, but to display the complementarity of languages and texts. The space between one language and another opens up a "third space" between original and translation, a utopian space that no longer means or expresses anything, but refers to a "reine Sprache," a pure language, an expressionless and creative Word containing all possible meaning. In his discussion of the pure language, Benjamin refers to a form which will have immense importance in his future work: the arcade.[4]

Benjamin uses the arcade in his later work as a cultural historian to represent an ambiguous urban space, neither inside nor outside, a passageway which is also a space of consumption, a new materialization of urban space. In the essay on translation, the arcade comes to represent literal translation (which he favours) as against interpretive translation. While literal translation proceeds word by word, interpretive translation uses as its unit the "sentence" or the "proposition." Because interpretive translation replaces and covers over the original, it is more like a wall. Because literal translation allows the form of the original to penetrate the translation, it is more like an arcade. "For if the sentence is the wall before the language of the original, literalness is the arcade" (Benjamin, *Illuminations* 79; see Nouss 25, 162). The glass roof allows light to flow through matter, just as the literally translated text is a transparent surface which allows the light of the original to fall onto the new version, creating an interplay of surfaces. The literal translator, like the historian, will use the figure of the arcade to write a new kind of history of Paris (Niranjana 119). Both translator and historian rely on the unexpected encounter of objects and words, the confrontation of languages and temporalities, to jar us into a renewed understanding of the present. The work of translation, like the work of history, provide forms through which the past and present "flash" into uneasy constellation.

The comma of translation points, then, to the work of both translator and historian in creating an interplay of surfaces, bringing together disparate realities. It can be seen as a pulse-point, drawing the languages together and separating them at the same time, gesturing toward a third term, the space between the "original" and its "afterlife" in a second language. The juxtaposition of English and French phrases across the comma points to translation as a movement which reveals, rather than conceals, difference. The first language does not disappear in favour of the second but persists, like some pesky ghost.

How does *My Paris* use the comma? What realms of meaning are suggested by this marker? At one point in her novel, Scott's narrator says, "Wanting to stay afloat. To stay out of categories. Moving back and forth. Across comma of difference. A gerund. A gesture" (107). The comma is not a moment of explanation or interpretation ("Avoiding interpretative, i.e. cause-and-effect narrative") (93), but a space in-between, a space of blurred categories and undecidability. Here alternatives are suspended, multiple realities come together, differences coexist. This is the space of the *act* of translation.

Increasingly recognized as a space carrying both "ethical and esthetic imperatives," the act of translation couples dislocation with the renewal of life. Translingual practice points not to abstract ideas of identity and equivalence, but to the "continua of transformation" that mark our experience of language and of history (Bhabha 200, 203).

From Paris to Montreal

As an anglophone writer living in Montreal, Gail Scott lives, as many of us do, "in translation." She gives to this situation, to this consciousness of negotiating across languages and communities, a broad range of meanings: not only the experience of daily existence in a multilingual neighbourhood, or sensitivity to the political battles of French against continental homogenization, but also the desire to affiliate herself with a writing community that gives priority to questions of form and language (see "Miroirs inconstants"). In her essays, Gail Scott has insisted on the influence of francophone writing in her attempts to develop a formally innovative writing style. This language-consciousness and writerly sensibility are shared by writers like Erin Mouré and Robert Majzels, who draw from their situation as English-language Montreal writers an opportunity to "see" and reshape language.

It is not entirely surprising, then, that all three writers use "langages" in their writing, or that Scott and Majzels have recently turned to translation. Scott has translated a novel by France Théoret, *Laurence*, and Majzels, two novels by France Daigle. In the cases of both Scott and Mazjels, the novels they have chosen to translate extend their own aesthetic choices. *Laurence*, for example, though it presents an apparently linear narrative, is quite radical in its form. The manner of recounting is highly unusual and lacking in a conventional point of view; the storyline is interspersed with a kind of authorial commentary, *ex cathedra*, which is both extremely precise and enigmatic. There is little lyricism in the text, and a constant sense of premature halts, a jerkiness which prevents intimacy with the character. There are many points of confluence between *Laurence* and *My Paris*.

For these writers then, translation and writing, though representing discreet activities, fall along a continuum.[5] Lines of linguistic tension traverse a variety of texts – novels, essays, translations – revealing pressure points where language and cultural difference, concepts of self and otherness, come to expression through modes of translation.

The Bridge over the Arno

Gail Scott's *My Paris* opens a space of translation

which tests the conventional boundaries of interlin-
gual transfer. Her text joins other contemporary practices of translation which are realigning territories of
cultural difference in Canada, as elsewhere. They do
so, I argue, in the name of a new function for translation. Rather than serving as a passage across two
discreet cultural zones, translation opens up an inter-
mediate space between them. This space could only
be called a bridge if we think of the medieval and
Renaissance bridges with their shops and dwellings,
the Ponte Vecchio in Florence and the Rialto in
Venice. These are not efficient slabs linking one place
with another, not spaces whose entire meaning is
consumed with the experience of transit. Rather, they
are passages cluttered with shops and houses, where
entire existences can be spent. These bridges bring
duration to the experience of passage. Like Babel,
according to Paul Zumthor, they speak of an experience which is interminable, *inachevé* (221). These
remnants of the past speak, in unexpected echo,
across time.

NOTES

1   This is a revised version of an essay written for a special issue
     of the translator's journal *Meta* 45.1 (avril 2000): 73-79. The
     original essay includes a discussion of the poetic dialogue
     created by Jacques Brault and E.D. Blodgett in *Transfiguration*
     (Saint-Hippolyte: Éditions du Noroît; Toronto: Buschek
     Books, 1999).

2   "The comma was just a nuisance. If you got the thing as a
     whole, the comma kept irritating you all along the line. If you
     think of a thing as a whole, and the comma keeps sticking out,

it gets on your nerves; because, after all, it destroys the reality of the whole. So I got rid more and more of commas. Not because I had any prejudice against commas; but the comma was a stumbling block. When you were conceiving a sentence, the comma stopped you. That is the illustration of the question of grammar and parts of speech, as part of the daily life as we live it" (Stein 319-320).

3   For remarkable and illuminating commentaries and re-translations of this crucial essay, see Alexis Nouss, ed., *Traduction, Terminologie, Rédaction* (1997).

4   Benjamin's mention of the arcade in this early essay on translation (1923) is prescient because he did not begin the Arcades Project until 1927; see Susan Buck-Morss, *The Dialectics of Seeing: Walter Benjamin and the Arcades Project* (Cambridge; London: MIT Press, 1989) 38.

5   The same could be said for a number of other Montreal poets and novelists who have used translation as an extension of their own literary projects. David Homel's association with Dany Laferrière is a case in point.

WORKS CITED

Benjamin, Walter. "The Task of the Translator." *Illuminations: Essays and Reflections*. Ed. Hannah Arendt. New York: Harcourt Brace Jovanovich, 1968. 69-82.

Bhabha, Homi. "Unpacking my Library . . . Again." *The Post-Colonial Question. Common Skies, Divided Horizons*. Ed. Iain Chambers and Lidia Curti. London; New York: Routledge, 1996. 199-211.

Burke, Carolyne. *Becoming Modern. The Life of Mina Loy*. Berkeley: U of California P, 1997.

Niranjana, Tejaswini. *Siting Translation*. Berkeley: U of California P, 1992.

Nouss, Alexis, ed. *Traduction, Terminologie, Rédaction. Études sur le texte et ses transformations. L'essai sur la traduction de Walter Benjamin*. X.2 (1997).

Scott, Gail. "Miroirs inconstants." In dossier "Ecrire en anglais au Québec: un devenir minoritaire." Ed. Lianne Moyes. *Quebec Studies* 26 (Fall-Winter 1999): 23-25.

——. *My Paris*. Toronto: Mercury, 1999.

Stein, Gertrude. "Poetry and Grammar." *Writings 1932-1946*. New York: Library of America, 1998. 313-336.

Théoret, France. *Laurence*. Trans. Gail Scott. Toronto: Mercury, 1998.

Zumthor, Paul. "La couleur des idées." *Babel ou l'Inachèvement*. Paris: Éditions du Seuil, 1997.

Paris, *Mon Amour*, My Catastrophe, or *Flâneries* through Benjaminian Space

DIANNE CHISHOLM

Anyway – returning to divan. And lifting heavy volume of B's *Paris, Capitale du XIXe*. From turquoise roxy-painted bedside table. Subtitle *Le livre des passages*. *Passagenwerk* in German. Not yet available in English. Therefore weighing the more delightfully on the wrists. Not a real history. Rather – vast collection of 19th century quotes and anecdotes. Initially seeming like a huge pile of detritus. But – on looking closer. More like montage. Possibly assembled using old surrealist trick. Of free association. I opening at contents' list. "A" – *Passages* – glass-roofed arcades, malls. Hawking 19th century's new imperial luxury. Juxtaposed on "B" – *Mode* – Each new season. Ironizing time. Next to "C" – *Antique Paris, catacombes, démolitions* – Paris's underpinnings. Pointing to "D" – *L'ennui* – Eternal return. Present tense of dandy. Hovering over "E" – *Haussmannisation, combats des barricades* – Haussmann's wide boulevards. Versus the people. Progress's double coin. Segueing into "J" – Poet *Baudelaire*. First modern. Peer of "M" – *Flâneur* – whose initial post-revolutionary languor not ultimately resisting rising capitalist market. "X/Y" – Marx – realism. Next to *Photography . . . Social Movements. Dolls. Automatons . . . A person could wander here for months.*

Gail Scott, My Paris 18[1]

Gail Scott's *My Paris* is a radical experiment in metropolitan realism and an exemplary production of queer urban space. Moreover, foregrounding the architectonics of its own construction, the novel is an illuminating demonstration of new narrative.[2] A new, pseudo-autobiographical make-shift form of storytelling, new narrative combines fiction and citation in an arresting mimesis of today's global city. The "Paris" of *My Paris* appears in concrete, minute and panoramic detail from the day-to-day perspective of a visiting writer who anxiously watches herself watching/walking the city in search of a subject for a novel. A fictive fiction-writer, Scott's narrator admires Paris's literary history. An anglo-Montréaler, she brings with her a calamity of paradoxical emotions with roots in subaltern paranoia, imperialist guilt, feminist anger, hedonistic desire, racial confusion, socialist melancholia, and lesbian frustration. The diary she keeps is, in part, an image of auto-ethnographic projection. It is also, unwittingly, a critical historiography of the Western capital of postmodern capitalism. What distinguishes Scott's fiction is her detour through Walter Benjamin's unfinished magnus opus, *Das Passagen-Werk*, the "theory-fiction" that constitutes his last and most ambitious attempt to image the epochal rise and fall of utopian capitalism. Scott's mimicry of Parisian phantasmagoria is mediated and subverted by her narrator's immersion in Benjamin's montage. A parodic, intertextual passage, *My Paris* revisits Benjamin's *Paris* before "arriving" at the city of now.

Scott's use of Benjamin is explicit. The text her narrator drifts into and is absorbed by is precisely identified as *Paris, Capitale du XIXe Siècle*, the French translation of *Das Passagen-Werk*. The narrator testifies as to how she comes upon this tome, left behind by the previous occupant of the writer's studio that she now inhabits. Impressed by its "weightiness," she scans its contents, immediately challenged to comprehend its representational device. The gesture of lifting the volume and browsing through its pages quickly becomes a habit, a morning ritual in her preparation for braving the traffic-choked, mesmerizing store-fronted streets outside her window. The more she reads, the more her perception of Paris is altered, the more visible become the material contradictions that underlie the collective illusion of Europe's still-most-dreamed-of-city. Her chronicle of walks is punctuated by crises of vision. Before the spectacle of Parisian cultivation, her nervous self-consciousness momentarily, and repeatedly, gives way to shocking recognition of devastated humanity, the price of capitalist "advancement" that the dream can no longer assimilate.

Though it handles "the heavy volume of B's *Paris*" with deceptive levity, *My Paris* sets the scene for activating one of modernism's most incisive strategies: the dialectical optics of Benjamin's image-space or "montage . . . using old surrealist trick. Of free association . . . Juxtapos[ition]." We would be mistaken to think of Scott's citation of *The Arcades Project* as postmodernist lampooning of modernist avant-garde invention. Instead, we might think of it as the enactment of a belated comprehension of what Benjamin/modernism attempted and never completed. Just as Hal Foster has recently hypothesized *"rather than cancel the project of the historical avant-garde, might the neo-avant-garde comprehend it for the first time?"* (15), Scott's narrator does not recover *The Arcades Project*, ironically, only to make her departure; *The Arcades Project* returns from the future, with unexpected timeliness, to guide her daily excursions into the capital of the late twentieth century.

Yet if *My Paris* "comprehends" Benjamin's *Paris* (the historical avant-garde) "for the first time," in an effort to re-present the real, historical Paris, then how do we understand the discovery by the former that the latter is "Not a real history" but a "surrealist trick," an "assemblage" of "juxtaposed" archival "quotes and anecdotes"? The concern that Scott shares with Benjamin is the problem of representing modern history without reproducing the spell-binding effect of capitalist phantasmagoria wherein "real" history is obscured. The problem is one of continuing emergency for the critical avant-garde. Benjamin recognized in Baudelaire a first attempt to use poetry as a technology of perception with which to grasp metropolitan contemporaneity, otherwise superficially experienced as a bombardment of shock. Does Scott recognize in Benjamin, if not an updating and adapting of Baudelaire, then a new use of surrealism to apprehend the antitheses of modernity and/or mirage of historicity that obscures our sense of reality today?

What is the task of the critic when the writing in question incorporates and performs the theory we might bring to its interpretation? In reading *My Paris*, her most obvious task is to determine how Scott's text uses Benjamin's theory/technique to "see" contemporary urban reality. The more subtle task entails querying and exploring the nature of the change which Scott's ("narrative") articulation of theory brings about: what other theory, thinking, critical/cognitive structures does *My Paris* assemble in its ability to comprehend Benjamin retrospectively? The larger, philosophical task entails inquiry into how *My Paris* affects and enhances our heavily mediated, radically atrophied perception of history. With these tasks in mind, the subsequent sections of this essay will review Benjamin's montage-historiography before analyzing the novel's comprehension and enactment of its theory/method. My reading of *My Paris* is thus selective, foregrounding figures and structures produced by the Scott/Benjamin relay, including the *flâneur*, the "dialectics of watching," and the allegory of the angel of history.

"Not a Real History"

The Arcades Project and related texts – the Baudelaire essays, the 1935 and revised 1939 exposés ("Paris, Capital of the 19th Century"), the "Theses on the Philosophy of History" – aim their avant-garde critique of capital specifically at the historicist-progressivist account of the post-revolutionary era. In Convolute N, "On the Theory of Progress, Theory of Knowledge" (*The Arcades Project* 456-488), Benjamin sketches out a method of "literary montage," of juxtaposing archival citations of contradictory testimony, without saying anything, just exhibiting, so that the myth of bourgeois progress is seen at once for what it really is: a mass of fragmented and colliding objects and intentions blended into fictions of cultural triumph. The montage method is variably deployed in the three essays composing "The Paris of the Second Empire in Baudelaire" (1938) and in "Some Motifs in Baudelaire" (1939), a revision of "The *Flâneur*," the second of the three essays. *The Arcades Project* could be interpreted as one massive montage, with a deep, axiomatic structure of imaging ideological antitheses across a panorama of metropolitan phenomena. But Benjamin's montage implies history-telling of a kind, even if the aim is to destroy capitalism's *grand-récit*.

The negative thesis of Benjamin's covert chronicle of history is the thinking that motivates the destructive impulse of his critical practice. It is useful to paraphrase this thesis to explain the analytical aim of his montage, though the practice of dialectical imaging resists simple explication. History, the story goes, began with the French Revolution. Rousing the collaboration of proletarian forces, insurgent bourgeoisie inaugurated a new social order based on change and idealized as "progress." Reason, industry and solidarity were to pave the way to commonwealth.

With new-found faith in industrial capitalism, the immovable edifices of divine rule were displaced by rapidly erected cornerstones of the bustling metropolis. Liberty, fraternity, and justice were drawn into the blueprints of "phalansteries" by the engineers of utopian socialism. But city building and capital growth became ends in themselves; proletariat revolution was waylaid and suppressed. New urban architectures and media technologies distracted, consumed and seduced the city's working inhabitants, converting "the people" into "crowds," amassing congregations under glass-domed arenas of commodity fairs. The luxury arcade became the city's centrepiece, a miniature globe wherein all the treasures of the empire – newly manufactured merchandise from adjoining factories, exotic artifacts from the colonies – were exhibited for mass consumption. Englobed in the space of the commodity, history itself becomes an exhibit and entertainment for public consumption.

If social transformation is blocked by the captivation of radical impulses in the phantasmagoric space of capitalism, then critical theory must invent a method of representation to "explode" this space and liberate revolutionary (cognitive) energies. Benjamin's montage of nineteenth-century Paris captures "dialectics at a standstill," striking the reader with a direct perception of antithetical forces mobilized by the bourgeois production of space. Montage replaces mythic history – the fairy tale of progress – with a concrete object, the arcade, that resembles the city in miniature and embodies the Ur-form of capitalist modernity. In montage, the object appears as an image: a primary dream image of the city's dreaming collectivity. A form of dream analysis, montage represents the dream, not by performing a secondary revision so that it figures as an artifact in the bourgeois narrative of progress, but by deconstructing the image into unassimilable fragments that resist the synthesis of explanatory reason/wishful thinking.

Benjamin's montage of nineteenth-century Paris, of the arcades, destroys the idea of the city as a social unit. Images (citations – blueprints, plans, sketches) of Fourier's *phalansterie*, comprising factory, residence and arcade for housing worker colonies, collide with images of proliferating consumption, of afterwork crowds circulating spellbound through passages of storefront displays. Images of republican fraternity clash with those of poor citizenry prohibited from entering the arcades' open doorway. Images of technological sophistication – engineering in iron and glass – contest those of labyrinthine corridors, uncannily echoing mythic prehistory. Images of promenading high society crash against those of mass prostitution.

In Benjamin's day, the arcade had long since been replaced with and reproduced on a grand scale by buildings of the Second Empire and *belle époque*. These included the *Bibliothèque Nationale*, the "dream house" where Benjamin constructed his *Arcades Project*, and the 1937 World Exposition, the industrial spectacle which captivated and dispersed the last of the revolutionary forces of the Popular

Front (see Ivernel). Today, all Paris is one, manifold arcade, featuring new "dream houses" like the *Forum des Halles boutiques* and *Centre Pompidou*, fantasy parks and science parks like *Disneyland-Paris* and *Parc de la Villette*, poshly renovated ethnic and/or working-class neighbourhoods like *le Marais*, *Belleville* and *Menilmontant*, all of which is crowned by *la Tour Eiffel*, iconic remnant of the World Exposition of 1889.

My Paris is a series of stops in a daily passage through the city over the course of six months. The city is the object of the narrator's strolling perceptions. More precisely, it is a collection of objects that she encounters, or spaces that she enters, as she sets about seeing. Objects of perception, they are transformed into images, which the narrator, fascinated, details in a diary. Since she trains herself to see the city in dialectical images modelled on Benjamin's *Paris*, *My Paris* records *flâneries* in Benjaminian space. A diary of passages, it chronicles encounters with the spectacle of history, historic Paris, while resisting the narrative of progress. A narrative that traces a perpetual breakdown of narrative, *My Paris* follows the official story of post-revolutionary history to where it collapses in ruined spectacles of imperialist/fascist capitalism before the *flâneur*'s expectant gaze. The novel's guerilla tactic of dialectical imaging is deployed in the narrative act of watching and writing. But in deconstructing capitalism's *grand récit*, it sabotages the diarist's own narrative intention.

The Return of the Flâneur

The *flâneur* is the protagonist of *My Paris*. She is a primary narrative strategy, a fictional device upon which the narrator herself reflects. The heroines of Scott's other novels, *Heroine* (1987) and *Main Brides* (1993), are also *flâneurs*. But the *flâneur* of *My Paris* is the only heroine to transform Benjamin's "*Flâneur*" into a narrative praxis. Moreover, the *flâneur*'s classical masculinity is altered by Scott's transgendering and transsexualizing, exploring and advancing Benjamin's analysis of the "erotology" of Baudelaire's *flâneur*. The *flâneur* of *My Paris* is a complex construction and adaptation of Benjaminian motifs.[3]

Flâneur of the Interior. In the opening scenes of *My Paris*, the narrator ponders her status as a visitor to the city, suspecting that she is "maybe already less of a traveller than a flâneur" (14). Thinking herself a *flâneur* gives her the sense of an occupation without committing her to a job. As a foreign visitor to Paris, she grants her alien status a literary character. But this act of identification is a pose that recalls the *flâneur*'s fictional nature. Literary historians question whether the *flâneur* actually existed or was an invention of the physiognomists and, later, the novelists (see Ferguson 26; Shields 62-63). Scholars agree, however, that the *flâneur* was a figure of bourgeois disaffection, a type of social drop-out who strolls the streets of the industrial capital against the accelerating flow of commercial traffic. He performs a comedy of tactical gestures that is aimed against capitalist earnestness, strolling through the arcades at a lobster's pace. Moreover, "in the *flâneur*, the joy of watching is triumphant" (Benjamin, "Modernism" 69). Acting the critical observer who refuses to harness consciousness to business or pleasure to work, the *flâneur* is the city's most devoted reader. A reader of *flâneur* literature (Balzac, Baudelaire), the narrator of *My Paris* enters the streets as the latest version of that tradition.

The latest version of that tradition is, as Scott's narrator exclaims, a "flâneur (of [the] interior!)" (14). Critics argue that it was precisely the interiorization of the *flâneur* that brought about his downfall (Ferguson 32). If, in the arcades of the Restoration, the *flâneur* strolls at a lobster's pace with eccentric *bonhomie* (26), on the boulevards of the Second Empire he dodges the traffic with grimacing heroics. The arcades constituted a haven for the *flâneur*, since there he could gaze with distracted ease while cultivating a pose of disinterested attention. As the ethic of industriousness advances, the *flâneur* loses his battle to stay aloof and afloat on the busy, commercial streets, diverting his strolls indoors like Huysmans's "aristocratic ex-dandy [Des Esseintes, who] withdraws from the city entirely ('so that the waves of Paris will no longer reach him'. . .) to devote himself to the systematic exploration of sensory and intellectual experience" (Ferguson 37). Or like Proust, who, unable to cope with the city's noise and pollution, retreats to his cork-lined bedroom to conjure ambling reminiscences (38). The withdrawal of the *flâneur* from direct city contact allegedly marks the defeat of the public artist (see Buck-Morss; Ferguson 35). Scott's narrator implies the defeat of a tradition. "But exhausted," she writes in her diary's short hand. "So late again when slipping off cushion. Clearly not flâneur. In later 19th-century sense of industriously strolling . . . Whereas *I* preferring to lie back in interior of peluche" (15).

Like Proust, she suffers from urban fatigue and seeks a cushioned retreat. Her desire to withdraw into her writer's studio is intensified in proportion to the intensified assault of late twentieth-century traffic on urban ecology. But there is no asylum. Despite her efforts to create sanctuary (flooding the studio with music from Maghreb on French radio or the aroma of freshly brewed espresso, dreaming that her window onto busy Boulevard Raspail overlooks a village meadow, returning to bed or sprawling on the divan with a romance by Balzac in mind), the studio is invaded by the morning's rush-hour traffic, by her concierge's brash intrusions, by drastic "repairs" to her studio walls. Unlike Proust, she cannot occupy luxury space without fearing she is undeserving. Though providing a cover for her insecurities, her *flâneur*'s masquerade is doubly pretentious: the prerogative of another era and another class.

Her motive for posing as a *flâneur* is not entirely known to herself. Having just arrived from "chez nous" (Montreal) to take up tenure as a writer, she is not yet sure of her literary project. She has trouble locating herself in Paris's intellectual and artistic milieu. As a *flâneur*, she is relieved of having to assume an ambition beyond watching the city, an (artistic) occupation in its own right. As a *flâneur* of the interior, she wanders into the city's cafés, pavilions and passages, drinking in the sensual ambience, floating over the barrage of traffic while remaining drunkenly aloof of social expectations.

Flâneur's Diary. The *flâneur*'s art is a fleeting one, an art of the moment, which is the art of the modern (see Baudelaire's *The Painter of Modern Life*). The *flâneur* sketches the city of his *flâneries* (Ferguson 30). Scott's *flâneur* watches Paris in freeze-framed scenes that she splices together like a cinematographer. Her diary is a direct citation of her visual montage. The aim of making her chronicle "more progressive" expresses the diarist's wish to overcome the author's reactive tendencies ("limitations," "biases"), which are both personal and political in nature. Assuming the guise of narrator, the diarist gives the pose of *flâneur* an explicitly artistic character, displacing the author as artist. The effect of this displacement is to relieve the narrator of prejudices and anxieties, leaving her free to wander. The *flâneur*-narrator is delivered from the tyranny of authorial "hang-ups," which do not disappear but comically surface in her physiognomies of the city.

It is well into her "diary" that Scott's diarist considers using a "narrator" to make her "chronicle" of *flâneries* "more progressive" by finding the device to mask her prejudices: "Me lying here thinking how to write. More progressive chronicle. Maybe author *déjà vu* by narrator. Instead of reverse. Permitting

latter to float beyond limitations. Biases. Of former"
(50). The diarist who entertains the idea of using a
narrator is already a *flâneur* who keeps a diary. In
stopping to think about how she might narrate her
flâneries, she alerts the reader to the illusion of direct
observation that preceded this point of the narrative.
In looking at her "chronicle" as a writer's diary, she
submits her *flâneries* to questions of "how to write."
Previous attention was focused on finding an idea for
a novel, the launching of which her retreat in Paris is
intended to facilitate. After drifting for several weeks,
she reveals a plan for a "book on murdered women
wanderers" (21) which she sends to prospective publishers. Her *flâneries* help pass the time while she
waits for word of acceptance. When she is met with
rejection, her *flâneries* suggest themselves as suitable
material for a novel, while the projected book on
murdered women wanderers proceeds to haunt the
narrative as a subtext.

The diary's narrator is not one with her pose as
flâneur and, thus, is unlike the classical *flâneur* who
is self-possessed in his social disaffection. He strolls
the city as a monad, whose insularity and detachment
is afforded by class privilege: a radical expression of
bourgeois individualism. Conversely, Scott's *flâneur*
is neither self-possessed nor naturally detached. Her
pose as *flâneur* does not make her Parisian, though
she eyes Paris with a longing to belong. She queries
the being-at-oneness with national identity that the
French exude, observing how the French language is
centred on "*On*" – the "I" of interpellated Republi-

canism. Artfully delivered of the author's hang-ups
with identity, however, the narrator is free to invent
a syntax and rhetoric of alterity and see things, not as
they seem, but as signs of the real. Looking back on
what she has written, she questions her own naïveté
concerning the veracity of direct reporting: "thinking I telling a lot of lies in this diary" (40). She
reflects on her own style of "watching" that negates
the practice of empirical observation while revealing
the catastrophic city behind a seduction of appearances.

Flâneur's Syntax. The writerly flâneur of My Paris
observes street life at linguistic street level, "watching
'verbs' " and citing what she watches in mimetic syntax: "I in a dream state. Ordering more espresso.
Before getting up and strolling. Toward asymmetrical
steeples. Of lovely Saint-Sulpice. Pausing. Watching
'verbs.' Pigeons. Nuns. Water blowing from four
bishops' fountain" (36). Syntax mimes the flâneur's
pace: slow, dreamy drifting, strolling and pausing,
with and against the pace of the city. The enjambment
of sentences reflects her ambiguous progress. Arriving
full-stop in midstream of a strolling perception, each
sentence refers back to the previous one, as well as
forward to the next. Stops break the flow. Objects of
predication are not structured around a subject but
are linked across sentences by association. A metonymic tracking mimes the mobile seeing of things-
becoming-images. The perceiving subject of these
images is neither transcendental ego nor synthetic
Idea. The flâneur's "I" (eye) is subject to a free

association of city-objects that are "no longer nouns but movement" (125).

Scott's jerky prose could imply *flâneur* kinesiology, adapted to the stopping and starting of city traffic (Benjamin, "Some Motifs" 119). The enjambment of sentences counters this automatism with thoughtful reflection. As a montage of signs, "watching" prompts seeing beyond the realistic frame that meets the eye:

> Watching – it occurring to me. Movement over square. Less real-time mirror. Than cinema of gestures. Pointing beyond frame. E.g. empty chair opposite. Possibly implying how "one" aching for her. Simultaneously expanding grammatically. To take in time's "progress." At margins of perception: guy on terrasse. Now kissing girl. Passionately. Tiny vans. Parking on narrow sidewalks. Economy of bustle. Keeping Paris going . . . (34)

Juxtaposing verbs (gestures) with the semiotics of dream, "one" perceives the hidden (libidinal) "economy" in the order of things.

"Watching . . . movement," Scott's *flâneur* is prompted to think of Gertrude Stein, whose English syntax imitates the French. At the same time, she glimpses "Stein miming" the "economy of bustle": "Keeping Paris going. Axed on verb. The French-language way. Which way Stein miming. Walking poodle Basket up windy Raspail. Trumpeting that by emphasizing predicates. She inventing the 20th" (35; see Stein, *Paris France* 12). The reflexive syntax of these perceptions implies that Stein, while miming "the French language way," goes with the flow of progressive enterprise (boulevard Raspail being a main thoroughfare of commercial traffic), and that her patent predication is a trumpeted invention of high capitalism. Mocking Stein's "trumpeting" in the *flâneur*'s physiognomic fashion, Scott caricatures Stein's attitude to Paris during the rise of American capitalism. Her speculations on "how to write" (50) allude not only to Stein's guide to radical composition, *How to Write*, but also to *Paris France*, whose narrative is predominantly descriptive and interpretative. Dwelling on this caricature, she begins "thinking of Stein's predilection for predicates. Which predicates – in multiplying – soaking up surroundings. Until mysteriously inflating subject (narrator). Into huge transparent shadow" (36). Against Stein's "predilection for predicates," Scott's narrator displays a predilection for present participles that, miming strolling perception, disperse the subject among objects of spontaneous association. Less like the pontificating and patronizing narrator of *Paris France* than the *flâneur* of Benjamin's "Hashish in Marseilles," Scott's narrator appears "stoned" (42) on a metonymic drift, subverting categorical (hierarchical) divisions between (enunciating) subject and (enunciated) object with strategic porosity.

Flâneur-Surrealist. The city is the classical *flâneur*'s true love. Disdaining the company of women, he goes to the arcades alone to enjoy the intoxicating display of goods and crowds. Likewise,

Paris allures Scott's *flâneur* who reflects that "more and more I loving it" (40), even "loving walking here" where "here" is rue de Rennes (125), choked with consumer traffic. But Scott's *flâneur* cruises as she flans (*flâner*), projecting desire onto attractive passers-by and fellow women travellers (invoked, without propriety, by their initials "S," "C," "P," "T"). Seeking a women-loving city as much as a prospective love affair, she indulges in dream-like distraction. At once auto-erotic and solicited, this distractedness is something other than the detachment with which the classical *flâneur* absorbs city pleasures. Passing as a *Parisienne* so as to be unnoticeable and yet charmed by the aura of fashion, Scott's *flâneur* must appear sufficiently modishly-feminine without succumbing to the tyranny of the mannequin. She tries not to take too much delight in looking good, in seeing her made-up self stylishly reflected in boutique windows, and to resist the gaze of commodity exchange occasionally signaled in men's appreciative glances. Nor does she abandon her wariness of danger in a city that murders women wanderers.

Yet, to achieve the presence of mind conducive to flan, she consumes a cornucopia of mild hallucinogens – mostly exquisite foods (espresso, lamb, cheese, wine) – losing herself in spaces flooded with savories and aromas, tones and images. Drifting across the city, she maintains her *ivresse* by absorbing the ambience of its gardens, squares, cafés, golden domes in the sunset, the Seine fairy-lit at night by passing *bateaux mouches*. This tactic of dream-walking was

things 'just keep going' as before *is* the catastrophe."[5]
Ellipses between diary entries are enjambed with the
refrain "raining [or snowing] in Bosnia," updating the
state of (the) war with the regularity of a weather
report. "Spleen is the feeling corresponding to catastrophe in permanence" (Benjamin, "Central Park"
34). Tragic newspaper stories are splenetically reiter-
ated, protesting the market's injunction to writers
that "to charm requiring anecdotes" (23). On her
daily drift through *Le Monde*, the *flâneur* encounters
uncharming anecdotes mostly involving immigrants:
"young Algerian professor is expelled" (30), "European indifference toward current horror in Bosnia.
[Traced] Back to centuries-old hatred Christian hate
of Muslims" (34), an African drowns in the Seine after
attempting to escape police inquiry (49), "Kenyan
athlete. Lacking visa like me. Jumping into Seine. To
save elderly Frenchman. In act of suiciding. One
month later Kenyan receiving *two* letters from préfec-
ture. One citing bravery. The other inviting him. To
leave country" (75), a Muslim youth is stabbed to death
by his peers, whose violence is attributed to the uninhab-
itable conditions of the housing project in which they are
forced to live (93), "Famous Zaïrois rumba singer.
Refused political asylum. Though wife dead mysteriously. Daughter 14 raped. Back in Zaïre" (105).

The allegory of catastrophe is literally the writing
on the wall. Drifting into the heart of *le Marais*, the
historic Jewish neighbourhood, now renovated with
delicatessens and boutiques (see Cobb), she is shocked
to encounter a holocaust memorial:

Walking. Walking. Repassing façade with two ring-
nosed heads of oxen on it. Carved message under: DE
CETTE ÉCOLE, 165 ENFANTS FURENT DÉPORTÉS
EN ALLEMAGNE PENDANT LA DEUXIÈME
GUERRE MONDIALE, ET EXTERMINÉS DANS LES
CAMPS NAZIS . . . Poem painted across neighbouring
delicatessen window. You can sow my ashes / On the four
corners of imbecility / No one will silence me. We de-
vouring plates of liver paste. Marinated vegetables. Delicious bread. Cold white wine . . . I starting raving . . . (67)

The diary's most elaborate allegorical refrain is
"ready-made." It is presented to the *flâneur* as a
found-object (*trouvaille*) in the display window of a
men's wear shop on boulevard Raspail. Arranged in
theatrical poses that are frequently rearranged, the
shop's mannequins hail the passer-by in stirring *tableaux vivants*. Dressed in black and choreographed to
imply the scene of a crime, their gestures reflect her
fears of male conspiracy:

> *Something strange going on there!* Mannequins in un-
> believably well-made suits. Handstitched lapels.
> Switching constantly. From window to window. Now
> one mannequin arm in knife-sharp cuff. Gesturing
> magnanimously to other. In neighbouring display win-
> dow. As if some kind of code. Or narrative. Generated
> by understanding. Men having between them. (33-34)

This theatre of mannequins displays the allegory of
commodity. Commodities are things whose meaning
fluctuates with the value placed on them by the
consumer market. To Benjamin, they are signs full of

phantasmagoric wonder, promising everything but symbolizing nothing, except the fallenness of a world that has lost sight of history and devalues both nature and culture. Allegorical vision is needed to see the allegory that is veiled in phantasmagoria – the erotic aura of consumer phantasy. The charisma of these mannequins dresses in masculine sadism, appealing to the heterosexual status quo. A later arrangement replaces the "magnanimous" coding of *Bruder-bonding* with ominous hints of *Lustmort*:

> Looking closer at display window across street. Seeing standing suit no longer wearing conspicuously striped square garb. Of elegant escroc, thief. But ordinary brown suit. Slightly fitted. Respectable. Except *2 red paper hands*. Emerging from *each* sleeve. As if bloody from strangling. (79)

The mannequins sell men's wear by spectacularizing male violence while a war is going on next door. The *flâneur* notes other contradictions. Images of homelessness are exploited (136), as are images of labour (90) in this collage of advertisement. Even poverty is selling. The last entry in her diary details an apocalyptic scene:

> In right display window – male hand rising. From pile of bunched up-coloured papers. Perfect sleeve or perfect coat. Holding tiny clock. While headless standing man in window to left. In dark pants. Shirred purple velvet vest. Pointing towards diminutive timepiece. In hand. Of window on right. (152)

In the *flâneur*'s re-presentation of the mannequins' charade we read a futurist allegory of triumphant right-wing conspiracy: the beheaded (guillotined) corpse is all that remains of the left's body politic.

The triumph of fashion over the needs of humanity can be read allegorically in the advent of the mannequin. The mannequin displaces the individual human body as a standardized physique. The moment that the body, initially the female body, is made to fit the mannequin's dress marks the ascendance of the inorganic over the organic (see Benjamin, "'B'–*Mode*" in *Paris*). We are shown this in the *tableaux* of the men's wear shop, where mannequins are figured as agents of murder. That the mannequins are dressed as men indicates that the male body is now a viable target of consumer display. In this war unto death, the *flâneur* unconsciously sides with the organic. At one point, a live rabbit is thrown into the installation as a prop. The terrified animal defecates over the display space, leaving little turds that the *flâneur* compares to her own – "his shit small and tight. Like mine" – noting that shit in Paris is "black from the soot," the city's toxic wastes (67).

The Dialectics of "Watching"

Using Benjamin's *Paris* as prosthesis, the *flâneur* of *My Paris* trains herself to see. Her training is less disciplined than impulsive:

B adding:
*Que les choses continuent comme avant: voilà la catas-
trophe.*
I taping it to TV screen. (68-69)

By removing the tape to watch the screen beneath,
she risks subverting her own tactic. At once concen-
trated and distracted, her presence of mind before the
television reflects the threshold receptivity that Benjamin thought most conducive to mass culture (see
Benjamin, "The Work of Art" 239-241). For her,
concentration is a play of distraction that she enacts
with comic self-consciousness. As if to demonstrate
Benjamin's thinking, she notes precisely the passage
concerning receptivity while still half-awake:

> On radio soft elegant woman's voice saying *France-
> Musique*. Then piano. Violin. Slipping back to dream.
> B saying threshold between dreaming and waking:
> ideal site for projecting past (dream). Into present
> (real). And reverse. Producing. Through shock of en-
> counter. Spark of illumination. Which dialectic move-
> ment. Actually deep kernel. Of montage history. (59)

The perceptiveness of *My Paris* is heightened by
paradox. Paradox is the product of dialectical seeing.
It is not the *flâneur* who sees dialectically but the
reader who finds her at the crossroads of shocking
contradictions. For instance, in one entry the *flâneur*
is "[s]itting in café at Sèvres-Babylone. I.e. at corner
of Exquisite China and Pursuit of Sensuous Pleasure.
Homeless guy selling *Macadam, Pavement*. By métro.
Thinking time to start wandering" (25). At an inter-

section presided by two boutiques (whose names underline the allegory of commodity), she sees a homeless man selling *Macadam* by the *métro*. What she does not see is what the juxtaposition of images implies. Sentence enjambment signals the reader to regard these images in relation to each other instead of fitting them into a sequence of accumulating meaning. The images relate antithetically. The nature of their contradiction is historical and political, which we might paraphrase thus: The homeless guy is an emblem of homelessness whose legacy begins with the modernization of Paris. The modernization of Paris is signalled precisely by the thing he hawks to live – *Macadam* – the material used to pave the city's first boulevards (see Berman 158-159). Driven through the slums, the boulevards displaced the poor onto the street. Absorbed by the boutiques that lined these boulevards, the bourgeoisie abandoned revolution. The poor, forced to attend to basic survival, sell what they can, stationing themselves at the city's most trafficked corners. But they are defeated by the *métro*, a modern mode of transport that does not run on paving stones.

Ironically, the *flâneur* never sees the paradoxicality of her own observations. But in her distraction, she notes the intersection of antitheses that constitutes Benjamin's montage. Prompted into wandering by a thinking that remains semi-conscious, she leaves it to her reader to interpret the dialectics of seeing. Every entry in her diary uses Benjamin's montage. Some entries thematize the use of montage overtly (see entries #8, #18, #44, and #70) but, more often, montage is translated into gestures of seeing as an aspect of *flânerie*. Benjamin transformed his *flâneur*'s practice when he went into exile. The method he develops in *The Arcades Project* is not watching but reading, or a method of sighting citation. The Paris he observes is cited in a montage of images which he draws from city archives. Scott's method of watching/writing the city is no less mediated. Her *flâneur* sees the city through the optic of Benjamin's dialectics, as well as the multimedia of television, film, radio, and newspapers, which makes direct experience impossible. But what she cites in her *flâneur*'s diary, she perceives on site – not in the archives but in the streets of Paris today.

The remainder of this section will focus on those entries that, to my mind, best demonstrate the critical acuity with which *My Paris* puts Benjamin's *Paris* into practice. The key to reading Scott is the key to reading Benjamin, which requires attention to the art of juxtaposing images. The juxtaposition of images displaces the chronology of events, which is foundational to historicism. Construction of the dialectical image entails collecting and assembling archival debris blasted from official history (Benjamin, "Theses" 263). How images are juxtaposed is suggested by the (imminent) object of history *to* the suggestible city subject whose crises of experience make her more sensitive to contradiction than reassured by continuity. Historical perceptiveness involves a fascination with the past that subverts a habituation to the present. Contradiction is the spark of illumination that reveals the site of historical repression, awakening a political presence of mind.

The *flâneur* first encounters the historic city at a "medieval music concert" in the "old thermal baths at hôtel de Cluny" (18). A "monument of medieval civil architecture" (*Paris. Guide Bleu* 537), the *hôtel des abbés de Cluny* envelops her senses in phantasmagoria, embellished by the "singing [of] high songs from early in millenium" (18). The melancholy of the ages makes itself felt, "surfacing" from the baths' "vaulted" depths and "echoing" in song "bouncing off thick sand-brick walls" (19). The music stays with her until the next day, when she enters the event in her diary. Through the aura of antiquity, she sees the muses of modernity. Her memory of strolling down rue de Grenelle *en route* to the concert now foregrounds the boutiques against the medieval chorus in a queer constellation "of mannequins singing praises to the highest peons of the mode. Kenzo. Yves St. Laurent. And I forget who." (18). The façade of fashion momentarily loses its power of seduction that keeps consciousness spell-bound in the present. In the clash of epochal images, fashion appears as cosmic placebo to the Eternal Return, "ironic antidote to perpetual melancholy" (19).

"*Musée Carnavalet.*" *My Paris* presents three city sites where history is the spectacle. They are: the *Musée Carnavalet*, the "*Âme au corps*" exhibition of nineteenth-century art and science held in the *Grand Palais*, and the wax museum, *Musée Grévin*, perma-

nently housed in *Passage Jouffroy*. The history represented in these spaces is a late modern production of
space: a material projection of current bourgeois
phantasy onto architectures of the interior. In these
spaces, historical consciousness is made on site, captivated and manipulated. In Benjamin's day, only the
Passages and panoramas produced history this way.
My Paris turns a Benjaminian eye on the phantasmagoria of contemporary renovation.

The *Musée Carnavalet* occupies former aristocratic residences, *l'hôtel Carnavalet* (the favourite
residence of Madame de Sévigné) and *l'hôtel Le
Pelletier de Saint-Fargeau*. Appropriated and redes-
igned by the city, these *hôtels* now contain the entire
history of Paris. *L'hôtel Carnavalet* guides visitors
through passages from the city's prehistoric origins to
the end of the seventeenth century. *L'hôtel Le
Pelletier de Saint-Fargeau* covers the Revolution to
the present day. "*Le plus parisien des musées de
Paris*," the *Musée Carnavalet* is a star attraction.
Guide Bleu points to the museum's "*ensembles décor-
atifs*" ("*lambris, plafonds peints, mobiliers, provenant
de divers édifices*"), which capture the evolution of
Parisian life "*depuis la Renaissance*" with an aura of
authenticity: "*une musée d'ambiance*" (753).

The *flâneur* narrates her stroll through the museum in a diary entry written as a letter. Addressed to
"Z," a young friend from *chez nous*, it begins with an
image of Madame de Sévigné sitting in what was once
the courtyard of *l'hôtel Carnavalet*, writing letters to
her daughter and "mocking fellow nobles" (52) with

feminist complicity. Her address to Z (alluding perhaps to the next generation – generation Z – of self-determining women) re-cites and re-frames the ideological architecture. Her stroll follows the museum's chronology ("*La Révolution et le premier Empire, salles 101 à 113*"; "*Paris dans la premiére moitié du XIXe siècle, salles 115 à 126*"; "*Paris du second Empire à nos jours, salles 127 à 145*") but subverts its use of space. Rushing through *grandes salles* devoted to cultural treasures, she lingers in passages containing revolutionary artifacts. The time she gives to Revolution displaces the space that official history gives to Empire, Restoration, and bourgeois consolidation.

The *flâneur*'s image of the museum displays the display wherein history is doubly contained – first by the palatial apartments, second by bourgeois closets and containers with which the original residences are redecorated – reflecting the end of revolutionary history "when populace taking comfort in cosy interiors" (52). Revolutionary memorabilia are encased with decorative care. Behind "glass doors of Second Empire cabinets" there are: "Shelves flagging objects projecting images of bloody exuberance. Sèvres saucer with man waving Marie-Antoinette's head. Man on plate gleefully collecting blood in basin. Gushing out from guillotined neck" (52). Only those artifacts that can be fit into the furniture of the interior are selected to represent the Revolution. Covered with the "*étui*" of bourgeois cosiness, their revolutionary value diminishes, while their exhibition value appreciates (see Benjamin, "I"– *L'intérieure, la trace* in *Paris*). Revolution's domestication can be seen in the conversion of bloody actuality into cartooned crockery made palatable for bourgeois cuisine. "Citizen Le Sueur's watercoloured cut-outs of citoyens and citoyennes" lampoon revolutionary visages in reassuring physiognomies of *bonhomie*: "patriotic women's club snug in bonnets. Marat on shoulders of supporters. Revolutionary army: sans culottes: apprentice butchers. Hunters. Citizens with placards: Vivre Libre Ou Mourir" (52). Overlooking the gangs of armed terrorists that arose among Jacobin women's clubs, the museum is seen collaborating with pre- and post-revolutionary patriarchal repression.

"Succeeding rooms" display "succeeding revolutionary waves" (52). Located in a "long narrow alcove" and "exposed offhandedly" are the artifacts of the Commune: "a few objects including plate for printing 'L'Internationale.' Plus painting of a pair of nice fat Paris rats. Communards eating during siege" (52). Dismayed by such abjection, she notes "a group of socialist ladies from Provence. Clucking embarrassed. Sympathetic" (52-53).

Moving through these passages, the *flâneur* encounters "more gold leafed drawing rooms. Wherein decades of struggle ending – under Bonaparte" (53). The museum continues into the twentieth century with rooms full of masterpieces of Parisian art. But history ends with the Second Empire after the defeat of the Commune. The Commune is the last mobilization of revolution. It marks the proletariat's lost hope for a "bourgeois-worker brotherhood" (52). Bypassing the Commune, the museum stresses imperial continuity ("under Bonaparte"), which goes hand in hand with bourgeois history "also ending on Proust's bedroom. On Haussmann's boulevard" (53). "Proust's bedroom" is a synecdoche of the next phase of bourgeois expansion, the *belle époque*, which, in reaction to the failure of the Commune, reproduces the Second Empire on a grander scale. That "Proust's bedroom" is juxtaposed on "Haussmann's boulevard" implies the withdrawal of the *flâneur*-writer from the city's commercial highways.

How does the dialectical image work? In place of a tour through the *Musée*, we are presented with a montage of images. Images appear in pairs: 1) "Second Empire cabinets" / "flagging objects . . . of bloody exuberance"; 2) "Citizen Le Sueur's watercoloured cut-outs of citoyens and citoyennes" / "social realism"; 3) "defeat or Thermidor" / "cosy interiors"; 4) "better barricades" / "bourgeois-worker phantasmagoria"; 5) "Bonaparte" / "gold-leafed drawing rooms"; 6) "Proust's bedroom" / "Haussmann's boulevard." The juxtaposing of images deconstructs the idea of historical continuity and foregrounds the illusion-making devices of political reaction. It also exposes the illusion of progress ("better barricades"), focusing on the defeat of the Revolution by "bourgeois phantasmagoria." The pairing of images forges a conjunction of disparate objects that illuminates the dialectical logic of historical materialism: in each pairing we see the aesthetic recuperation of revolutionary history re-enacted in the museum's containment of Revolutionary artifacts ("Sèvres saucer with man waving Marie Antoinette's head") in bourgeois showcases ("Second Empire cabinets").

Scott's montage of *Musée Carnavalet* compares with Benjamin's 1935 exposé, "Paris, Capital of the 19th Century," which is composed of six pairings of juxtaposed images ("Fourier or the Arcades," "Daguerre or the Dioramas," "Grandville or the World Exhibition," "Louis Philippe or the Interior," "Baudelaire or the Streets of Paris," "Haussmann or the Barricades"). Benjamin focuses on the collective phantasmagoria of arcades, panoramas, world exhibitions, bourgeois interior, boulevards, and associated "stars" (the famed architects of this epoch) through which revolutionary forces are seen to arise. He breaks up the traditional chronicle of progress into a montage of phases of city development, re-presented as expanding architectures of capitalist dreamspace. He orders these phases to imply a passage of history that proceeds dialectically and "ends" with an image of the barricades raised against the boulevards (see Higonnet et al). Scott's montage ends less hopefully with Proust's bedroom on boulevard Haussmann. At this point her narrator asks whether Proust's style of writing would have been altered had the Commune won. Looking back at the luxurious comfort in which he composed, she answers negatively "why not," implying that bourgeois-worker solidarity was already lost to "cosiness" before the Commune's defeat.

Not to be framed by this phantasmagoria, the *flâneur* continues to wander, "leaving museum by rue des Francs-Bourgeois" which, she notes, was "named for hostel of bourgeois in early 17th c – still too poor to tax" (53). She steps into *le Marais* – the heart of tourism – where she has a memory of herself as a girl, a tourist, hitchhiking through the Alps with a bourgeois "couple," who invite her for a drink. She remembers acting out over sherry, opening her legs so that the man sees the blood stain from her "overflowing period." Perplexed by the spontaneity of this memory, she punctuates the scene with a question "why?" (the only question in the diary to be awarded punctuation), signalling both unconscious sympathy with the "period" of revolution overflowing with blood on streets that have fallen into bourgeois possession and feminist solidarity with the woman of the "couple" who is terrorized by her husband's reckless driving.

" *L'Âme au corps'* – *Grand Palais*." Diary entry "100" retraces the *flâneur*'s stroll through the "*Âme au corps, Body and Soul exhibit*" (127) of nineteenth-century art and science. The exhibit is housed in the *Grand Palais*, which is itself an item of exhibition, built for the 1900 World Fair. The theme of the exhibit is the artistic imagination of nineteenth-century technology and enlightenment, which has been captioned for the amusement of late twentieth-century spectators. As she sees it, the exhibit reinvokes precisely the phantasmagoria it gestures to dispel with curatorial hindsight. Her narrative displays the display of history and the ideological (re)production of space where learning is intended to take place. First, she reflects on the "Palais façade":

> ACADEMIC. Arts and sciences marching over. In mythological tropes. Basin with sylphs. Angels. Pineapples. Horses. Prancing towards pont Alexandre-III's ornate cast-iron lamps. Pillories with golden-winged steeds. Golden alley. Rolling towards Napoléon's gold-leafed tomb. Behind Invalides. (126-127)

A monument to modernity, the building is decorated in *art nouveau*, which, paradoxically, is a recasting of antiquity. Modern arts and sciences are represented in figures of prehistory: enlightenment is manifested in mythology. From the *flâneur*'s perspective, modernity points backwards to *l'ancien régime* (Monarchy) and classical history (Empire) – antiquated forms of political history that were to become the future of modern revolution.

Inside, she feels unprecedented exposure to projections of the past "like none other ever having" (127). The space she enters is "uncanny" (127), reflecting the borderline psyche of the nineteenth-century mind. She imagines herself "wandering . . . in Dr. Freud's atelier. Where 'one' confronting past (unconscious)" (127). She foregrounds Benjamin's observation that capitalist enlightenment is a form of collective dreaming. The (unconscious) desires and fears of the ascendant bourgeoisie dominate this dreaming and are projected onto inventions and discoveries with apparent objectivity. Science collaborates with art to produce a dream technology. Her re-presentation of these nineteenth-century productions deploys montage to reveal the exhibition's "unconscious optics" (see Benjamin, "The Work of Art" 237). Species of nineteenth-century zoology appear as "androids" in taxonomic chimeras that combine animal and human features. Instruments of early nineteenth-century medicine appear as instruments of torture. In every image of advanced technology she perceives a counter-image of barbarity, noting the racism in the "progressive" methods of human science:

> Toward site where early photo technology. Joining early psychoanalysis. In murals of countless tiny mug shots. "Representing" criminal "types." Interpolated in "oriental" fold of eye. Sloping forehead. Pointy teeth. Signalling untoward animal instincts. (127)

What she reflects distractedly is that the dialectic of enlightenment is structured by the logic of the uncanny. Early photography becomes the instrument of early psychoanalysis, whereby external signs (the contorted body) are read as internal symptoms (the hysterical psyche). Early psychoanalysis lends its technology to criminology that produces racist physiognomies which equate criminality with oriental "animality."

In every scientific advancement we see the return of the repressed, an unconscious projection of the fear of the "other" onto subjects – the working class, women, immigrants – that the bourgeois republic (unconsciously) desires to subdue and exploit. The *flâneur*'s constellation of images captures "dialectics at a standstill," citing (sighting) the reactionary and exploratory simultaneously:

> Nineteenth[-century] passion for technology. Frequently leading to premature (reactionary) synthesis. But also to Redon's unfathomable watery painted figures. Sliding out of gaze. Or to Courbet's sleep investigations. Two fabulous naked women slumbering. In each other's arms. (127)

For Scott, as for Benjamin, the negativity of dialectical history is not totally nihilistic (as it is for Adorno and Horkheimer). Reactionary synthesis is countered by revolutionary possibility. New artistic technology discovers new human frontiers: the "unfathomable" unconscious and "sleeping" lesbian potentiality. Conversely, enlightenment thinking undergoes negative transformation. "Waking post-Commune" (127), the nineteenth-century subject sees the world through traumatized reason, whose symptomatic products are scientific scepticism ("doubting reliability of species. Which doubt fostering 'modern' psychiatric ward") tempered by capitalist rationality. We see the former in a caricature of Freudian analysis: "Wherein master himself pacing. Narrating someone else's dream. Being someone else's: even more impossible to pin down. Resultant shock. To 19th-century mind. Ultimately spawning surrealism" (127). We see the latter in the arrangement of the exhibition itself: "The whole sublimated. Analyzed. Summed up in little captions. Offering for consumption: 19th century subject" (127).

Montage displays the uncanniness of nineteenth-century inventions which continues to fascinate the twentieth-century curator. It also displays how the twentieth-century mind rationalizes its fascination using commodity's allegorical form ("little captions") to analyze, summarize, and present for consumption. The exhibition is intended *not* to awaken the dreaming collectivity but to entertain the individual spectator. The result is a kind of "grizzled feast having been laid out for 'one's' unique consumption. Orchestrated by aura-conjuring hand of curator" (128; see Benjamin, "The Work of Art" 233-234).

The exhibition works on the *flâneur* like a charm. She races to *Champs Élysées* "feeling certain marvellous to be had" (128). What she encounters are "rows and rows of cops blocking boulevard. Probably another demonstration" (128). The social reality of political reaction blocks the dream of revolutionary surrealism. In her *faux pas* we see that repression is the modus operandi of the bourgeois state and that public demonstration is the return of the repressed, eternally and ineffectually re-enacted (see entries #103, #106, and #111).

"*Musée Grévin – Passage Jouffroy.*" Another nineteenth-century dream house, the wax museum transforms the art and science of physiognomy into devices of historical spectacle. *Musée Grévin* exemplifies this transformation, demonstrating the decadence of *belle époque* phantasmagoria. An illusion of historical reality, the wax museum lacks the spell-binding power of the uncanny because the technology of reproduction is so blatant. Physiognomy is applied to the faces of the past in spooky caricature. The trick is to resurrect the dead of collective memory while lightening the burden of history.

Musée Grévin is located in *Passage Jouffroy*, one of the few remaining unaltered arcades. Housed within the Ur-form of capitalist dream houses, the *Musée* multiplies the effect of interiorization. The arcade reproduces the city in miniature with its gas-lit streets and shop-lined promenades. In turn, the wax museum reproduces the arcade to set the stage for recasting world history. Museum corridors guide visitors past dioramas of history's most memorable scenes – frozen in time but animated by the passage of spectatorship. The series of dioramas extends the technology of the panorama that was first used by city visionaries to bring the expanding parameters of modern Paris entirely into view. Surveying the commonwealth of urbanization, the view was utopian while being instrumental in cultivating bourgeois imperialism. The wax museum marks a further development in the use of optical illusion to globalize capitalist vision.

The *flâneur* encounters the *Musée* near the end of her wanderings. Her stroll through its haunts recaptures previous strolls through the Paris Passages (where she absorbs nineteenth-century ambience [138-139]), *Musée Carnavalet* (where she witnesses Paris history on display), and the *Âme au corps* exhibition (where she witnesses the nineteenth-century mind on display). Having been sensitized to the productions of bourgeois phantasmagoria, she is less absorbed than amused:

> Grévin a scream. Distorting mirrored labyrinth. Presenting history backwards. Modern retreating toward medieval. Starting off with Fonda. In *Barbarella* space suit. Surprised multiple orgasm expression of 1960's film. On physiognomy. Michael Jackson moonwalking. Backwards. Towards Communards. Napoléons. Jacobins. Several Louis. And queens . . . Head of some noble on pole. Being waved by victorious sans-culotte at incestuous lesbian Marie-Antoinette's window. She falling naturellement in faint. (140)

The museum moves backward in time but history is framed in the space of contemporaneity. The *flâneur*'s narrative of this passage displaces an impression of continuity with the disjunction of montage. In montage, the image of Fonda is ironically juxtaposed against the image of Marie-Antoinette. If Barbarella's "liberated" physiognomy caricatures the climax of modernity, the Queen's "shocked" physiognomy caricatures the *ancien régime*, revolutionized by terror. In the clash of images we see the spectacular repression of lesbian sexuality, implying that the age of (sexual) revolution is as "backwards" as ever.

Less focused on the drama than the "pallor of the sculpting material," she regards the spectacle allegorically as the commodity of history: "Giving almost cartoon effect. For contemporary viewer. Who further aware. Head of one hero often replaced by another. On reclad body. According to vicissitudes of public opinion" (140). Behind the masquerade of progress, she sees the mechanics of illusion that operate capitalism's eternal reproduction of the same. The museum displays its own construction, she observes, noting:

> Labyrinth ending in Palais des Mirages. Small room. Belle-époque. Columns of entwined snakes. Masks. Lights going out. Darkness slowly filling with lit-up butterflies. And stars. Stiffly rising. Descending. On faintly visible wires. "Beautiful." But technology so dated. Being chiefly conceived. Like old panoramas. For spectators. Watching from immovable center. (140)

The spectacle fails to fascinate the *flâneur* who watches from a displaced centre. As "one" whose desires are nowhere represented, except by the scandalously lesbian Queen who is beheaded and betrayed by agents of revolution, she is alerted to misrepresentation and falsifying devices. As phantasmagoria, the *Palais des mirages* is an inferior production (see Cohen 232-235). She is less affected by it than by the phantasmagoria she discovers in *Hôtel Chopin* opposite the *Musée*. Enjoying a revival among gay patrons, the *Hôtel* recaptures the seductive aura of the arcades.

> We glimpsing dark pink lobby. Campy lampshades. Men coming downstairs. We entering café with real wicker chairs. Opposite Grévin. With handsome male waiters. Little red kerchiefs knotted round necks. To drink fine porto. Out of lovely porto glasses. Beige palm trees in relief. Climbing up the wall. R taking in

male fauna. I the porto. Sinking by osmosis. Into roof
of mouth. (140-141)

From *Musée Grévin* to *Hôtel Chopin*, the *flâneur*'s
stroll through nineteenth-century arcade moves from
decadence to renovation. Yet the progress of this
passage is unclear. *Hôtel Chopin* is ambiguously im-
aged as the site of perverse emancipation where pa-
tron-worker exchange is intoxicated by the sexual
charisma of the marketplace. "Male fauna" is cast
among exotic flora. She is not entirely seduced but
her gay friend is infatuated. Through her eyes we see
gai Paris undergo its latest transfiguration. But is it
(gay) revolution or the eternal return of the same?

Angelus Novus: Angela Lesbia

Scott ends her six-month *flânerie* in Paris with a break
of uncertain time followed by a return. The last diary
entry figures her *flâneur* back home "trudging in
snow down Saint-Denis. Montréal. Québec" (152),
absorbing the discrepancies of social space. Two
pages later, she is once again in Paris, drinking in the
ambience of a New Year's eve in a "dark overcrowded
square" near Notre-Dame "[l]ooking toward (fog-
erased) Grand Palais" (155). Paris is, then, recorded
in a whirlwind of passages, where, in place of diary
entries, are paragraphs separated and joined by spaces
and dashes – long dashes, one passage leading into
another with acute acceleration. Instead of an ending,
we are given a coda, a formal device that functions

here, like in music, as "a passage added after the natural completion of a movement, so as to form a more definite and satisfactory conclusion" (*OED*). At once repetitive and visionary, the coda stages a final *flânerie* that, drifting as before but at an accelerated pace, exchanges catastrophe-ridden glances for glimpses of utopia. At the head of this run-on *flânerie*, the times are noted auspiciously as "New Year's 199_." The return of the *flâneur* is heralded by a title page, whose caption, lifted from an exhibition currently showing at *Centre Pompidou*, reads "*Le Sexe de l'Art*," marking the dawn of a new, queer epoch.

The coda, like the diary, is punctuated by reports on the ongoing war in Bosnia: war is the state of emergency that raises spectres of crises through the mists of phantasmagoria with unheeded alarm. The war is no less present in the coda, though in the fog-drenched streets of a Paris January at the end of the millennium, its presence is felt more directly:

> – Sauntering – Silent – Sky . . . Out into street. Dog-catcher truck. Buses – Taxi. Cruising past Odéon columns. Actors fasting. For Sarajevo – Leaving enclave. Dissatisfied – Suburbs – Cement saucer of airport – That dogcatcher truck. Pulling up behind. Woman stepping out . . . Saying I come from war. And here is confusion. Handing out pamphlet. Saying les Bosniennes, Bosnian women. Saving culture. In chaos. With 100 small attentions. Presenting themselves impeccably. Best food. In worst situations – Pink lips ahead. Pointed boots forward. Towards boarding gate – I turning. Once. Looking – (161)

The last image to be added to the constellation of *My
Paris* is a dialectical image. At once, looking ahead /
looking back, the *flâneur* presents a Janus-faced
glance at contemporaneity. What she sees is not a
spectre of hope or ruin but a real woman, from
Bosnia, bringing tidings of resistance. Against catastrophic "chaos" she beholds a figure of salvation, a
collective image of "les Bosniennes . . . [s]aving
Culture." But the realism of this image is animated by
a dream-wish, the dream of social transformation that
revolutionary modernity induces. On the outskirts of
the city, past the historic centre (where actors stage a
fast for the war), past the dismal, sprawling suburbs,
onto Charles de Gaulle Airport, the *flâneur* is borne
by a cumulative vision of unactualized possibility
beyond all materialized disappointment. The capacity
to see utopia is, Benjamin observes with retrospective
foresight, the affirmative dimension of metropolitan
phantasmagoria. Veiling catastrophe and sidetrack-
ing revolution, phantasmagoria also harbours a wish-
fulfilling impulse to transform. In the end, Scott's
flâneur is invested with this impulse.

   But in the coda, a new intoxicant has been added
to the dream in her drift through Paris. That intoxicant is erotic, lesbian, love. Paris is still a primary
passion of the *flâneur* who, on return from Montréal,
picks up where she left off, re-engaged. But her
engagement with the city is affected by the presence
of a lover who joins her from Canada. "Love" scores
the text both figuratively and syntactically. Where
there were once only periods there are now, peri-

odically, "orgasms," crossed out as perverse slips of speech:

> She beside me saying. Very pink lips. Initially not wanting to come. Preferring riding horses – Still what orgasms angels popping up. Mid walls. Near Louvre's small eyes. Looking in. Or out. She asking – (155)

Though reluctant to visit Paris, preferring more amazonian adventures, the lover is the cue to the *flâneur*'s final revelation. "Pink lips" appears "ahead" of the *flâneur* like a star on the horizon, illuminating the erotic orientation of the scene, "pointing forward" in a gesture that confirms that the future is women.

"Pink lips" appears in every coda passage as a corporeal gesture. A synecdoche of the lesbian body, she, like all bodies caught in the *flâneur*'s field of cruising, is erotically moving. An unassimilable fragment of (lesbian) sexual difference, however, "Pink lips" defies commodity fetishism that, as Benjamin notes, is the charismatic appeal of "the girl with the golden eyes." Nor is she like the dispensable Nadja, Breton's esoteric love with whom the surrealist *flâneur* is less intimate than the marvellous things she connotes. For Scott's *flâneur*, "she" is "she beside me" (155) who, in arousing proximity, initiates the metonymic drift that constitutes a lesbian semiotics. If, as Benjamin perceived, the "sexual shock" to which the big-city dweller is subjected is the violent effect of the commodity's division and appropriation of *sex* from Eros ("Some Motifs in Baudelaire" 125) then their unmarketable, lesbian, re-union is our redemption.

A figure also of communication/communion between women, "Pink lips" is the *flâneur*'s closest
interlocutor. When accompanying her on *flâneries*,
"Pink lips" speaks her desire, proposing alternatives
to "femmes légitimes" (155), ridiculing "Natalie
Barnie" (158), Paris's only "out" lesbian, and protesting the marginality "of girls like us" (159). Laughing
at the cowboy drag of Parisian gays (158), she mocks
their simulation from the perspective of real cowboy
knowledge (155). Like the horse-riding amazons of
Cirque d'Hiver (159), her androgyny contests the
gender status quo that Paris so artfully and artificially
preserves.

"Pink lips" signals "orgasms," that keep "popping
up" in the text, reflecting her subliminal affect on the
flâneur. Thinking "orgasms," she sees "angels"
sculpted into the Louvre's baroque façade – "mid
walls" (155). These imaginary, or visionary, angels
suggestively allude to Benjamin's angel, or the seraphic motifs in Baudelaire that he reads as figures of
baroque modernism. Scott tempts us to read her
orgasmic angel as a perverse and provocative adaptation of Benjamin's theses on the future of history.

Benjamin's most famous allegory – "the angel of
history" – takes Klee's *Angelus Novus* as referent. For
Benjamin, Klee's angel looks "toward the past" where
he sees catastrophe "piling wreckage upon wreckage"
("Theses on the Philosophy of History" 257). The
angel "would like to stay, awaken the dead, and make
whole what has been smashed"; but he is caught in a
storm "blowing from Paradise" that "irresistibly pro-

pels him forward into the future to which his back is turned, while the pile of debris before him grows skyward . . . The storm is what we call progress" (257). Benjamin, moreover, characterizes this Janus-faced angel of history as androgynous, alluding to "sources in the Jewish kabbalist tradition in which God is feminized, bisexualized" (Buci-Glucksmann 114), as well as sources in Baudelaire to whom prostitutes and lesbians appear as seraphic androgynes. Reappraising Baudelaire's idealization of outcast women in materialist terms, Benjamin explains that the prostitute of *Les Fleurs du mal* is angelic because she displays the "holy prostitution of the . . . commodity-soul" ("The *Flâneur*" 56) and because she affords the insular, alienated big-city dweller a form of "communing with the masses" ("Central Park" 40). As regards the lesbian, "the woman who bespeaks hardness and mannishness" ("Modernism" 90), she is angelic since she signals sexual purity even as she is socially damned. Benjamin discovers this *amour pur* of lesbianism to be a primary motif of *Jugendstil*, "Modern Style":

> The Lesbian woman carries spiritualization (*Vergeistigung*) into even the womb. There she plants the lily-banner of "pure" love, which knows neither pregnancy nor family. ("Central Park" 43; *The Arcades Project* 558)

To the lesbian's angelicism, Baudelaire adds her heroicism. *"The lesbian is the heroine of modernism,"* Benjamin reiterates, explaining "why Baudelaire for

a long time had the title *Les Lesbiennes* in mind" for
Les Fleurs du mal ("Modernism" 90; emphasis
added). Benjamin reads this heroism as a resistance to
the "impotent" ruling class, which, having "ceased to
concern itself with the future of the productive forces
unleashed by themselves," consoles itself with the
lame "idea of a pension" and "wish to have children"
("Central Park" 37). Recognizing that these tropes
should not be mistaken for Baudelaire's commitment
to women's emancipation, Benjamin attributes the
poet's sources to utopian socialism whose manifestos
were "in the air," in particular, those of Claire Démar:

> In the widely ramified literature of the time which
> deals with the future of women, Démar's manifesto
> [*Ma loi d'avenir*] is unique in its power and passion . . .
> Here the image of the heroic woman which Baudelaire
> absorbed may be seen in its original version. Its lesbian
> variant was not the work of the writers but that of the
> Saint-Simonian circle. ("Modernism" 91)

In recovering these sources, Benjamin documents a
forgotten, lesbian feminist, dimension of revolutionary history. Connecting the Saint-Simonians to "the
Vésuviennes" whose movement "supplied the February Revolution with a corps of women" (94), Benjamin conjectures that "such a change of the feminine
habitus brought out tendencies which were capable
of engaging Baudelaire's imagination." If the poet
"reached the point where he gave a purely sexual
accent to this development" (94), Benjamin reaches
further, resurrecting the political alongside the sexual

with a retrospective glimpse of the coming community of women.

At least one scholar has recognized the radical implications of Benjamin's otherwise untheorized speculations on female culture. "Female culture is ultimately universal culture," Christine Buci-Glucksmann writes, which makes it possible to confront difference within the self and the other. In this respect, we should bear in mind Benjamin's words:

> All rulers are the heirs of those who conquered before them. Hence, empathy with the victor invariably benefits the rulers. Historical materialists know what that means. Whoever has emerged victorious participates to this day in the triumphal procession in which the present rulers step over those who are lying prostrate. (88)

Buci-Glucksmann urges us to not overlook the mystical dimension of the "angel of history" in our focus on the allegorical. If read in light of Benjamin's kabbalistic sources, his "angel" becomes a visionary rendering of history's repressed potential – a feminine, androgynous and bisexual potential to absorb the fragmentation that issues from the sexual division of labour and commodity fetishism. And, if read in context of neglected historical sources in women's revolution, Benjamin's "angel" takes on a lesbian face. It is the lesbianism of utopian socialism that commands a change in "feminine habitus" so radical that woman should love her fellow woman as much as her fellow man, "mak[ing] it possible to confront difference within the self and the other" without hegemony.

Benjamin's reclamation of the revolutionary history of women is not lost on the poet-*flâneur* of postmodernism. The last image of the constellation of *My Paris* is an image of women, "Bosnian women," who emerge from history's ongoing catastrophe, "[p]resenting selves impeccably," while attending others "[w]ith 100 small attentions." Women's culture, were it to survive its repeated defeat, is (a) "[s]aving culture." Or so Scott's *flâneur* urges us to see, with the clarity of a vision prompted by love of woman for woman.

NOTES

1   The full version of this essay appeared in *Canadian Review of Comparative Literature/Revue Canadienne de littérature comparée* 27.1 (March 2001).

2   "New narrative" refers to a genre, or a movement, of experimental writing that explores and exhibits techniques of "narrativity" in the act (narrative present) of storytelling. The representational function of narrative is supplemented and interrupted by theory-based interrogation of the political economy of writing. Compounding fiction, politics and autobiography, new narrative plots a construction of the "self" by a language-sensitive narrating subject. The subject – invariably "queer" – is a vehicle of awareness of the big-city dweller's exposure to/seduction by urban commodity life. The "self" that is created in response to this life is a precarious object of desire and exchange.

3   Except where otherwise indicated, my thinking on the *flâneur* derives from Walter Benjamin, "The *Flâneur*," middle section of "The Paris of the Second Empire in Baudelaire," in *Charles Baudelaire: A Lyric Poet in the Era of High Capitalism* and

from *Konvolut* "'M'–Flâneur" in *Paris, Capitale du XIXe Siècle*.

4   In the eighteenth century a *grisette* referred to a working-class woman who wore cheap grey dresses; by the early nineteenth century it had come to mean a working-class woman who struggled to make ends meet by lifting her skirts at the end of a work day. Benjamin alludes to her throughout *The Arcades Project* as a working-class hero.

5   *"Que 'les choses continuent comme avant': voilá la catastrophe."* Benjamin, "'N' – *Réflexions théorique sur la connaissance, théorie du progrès*," *Paris* 491. Also cited in "Central Park" (50).

WORKS CITED

Adnan, Etel. *Paris, When It's Naked*. Sausalito, CA: Post-Apollo, 1993.

Balzac, Honoré de. *History of the Thirteen*. ["Ferragus"; "The Duchesse of Langeais"; "The Girl with the Golden Eyes."] Trans. Herbert J. Hunt. Harmondsworth, U.K.: Penguin, 1974.

Baudelaire, Charles. *The Painter of Modern Life and Other Essays*. Trans. and ed. Jonathan Mayne. New York: Phaidon, 1964.

——. *Paris Spleen*. Trans. Louise Varèse. New York: New Directions, 1970.

Benjamin, Walter. "Central Park." *New German Critique* 34 (Winter 1985): 32-58.

——. "The *Flâneur*." From "The Paris of the Second Empire in Baudelaire." [1938] *Charles Baudelaire: A Lyric Poet in the Era of High Capitalism*. Trans. Harry Zohn. London: Verso, 1983. 35-66.

——. "Hashish in Marseilles." *Selected Writings. 1927-1934*. Volume 2. Trans. Rodney Livingstone et al. Ed. Michael Jennings, Howard Eiland and Gary Smith. Cambridge, MA: Harvard UP, 1999. 673-679.

——. " 'M'–The Flâneur." *The Arcades Project*. Trans. Howard Eiland and Kevin McLaughlin. Cambridge, MA: Harvard UP, 1999. 416-455.

——. "Modernism." From "The Paris of the Second Empire in

Baudelaire." [1938] *Charles Baudelaire: A Lyric Poet in the Era of High Capitalism*. Trans. Harry Zohn. London: Verso, 1983. 67-101.

——. "Paris, Capital of the 19th Century." *Charles Baudelaire: A Lyric Poet in the Era of High Capitalism*. Trans. Harry Zohn. London: Verso, 1983. 155-176.

——. *Paris, Capitale du XIXe Siècle: le livre des passages*. Trans. Jean Lacoste. Paris: Les Éditions du Cerf, 1989. [*Das Passagen-Werk*. Frankfurt am Main: Suhrkamp Verlag, 1982] [*The Arcades Project*. Trans. Howard Eiland and Kevin McLaughlin. (Prepared on the Basis of the German Volume Edited by Rolf Tiedemann). Cambridge, MA: Harvard UP, 1999.]

——. "Some Motifs in Baudelaire." [1939] *Charles Baudelaire: A Lyric Poet in the Era of High Capitalism*. Trans. Harry Zohn. London: Verso, 1983. 107-154.

——. "Surrealism." *Selected Writings. 1927-1934*. Volume 2. Trans. Rodney Livingstone et al. Ed. Michael Jennings, Howard Eiland and Gary Smith. Cambridge, MA: Harvard UP, 1999. 207-221.

——. "Theses on the Philosophy of History." *Illuminations: Essays, Aphorisms, Autobiographical Writings*. Ed. Hannah Arendt. Trans. Harry Zohn. New York: Schocken, 1969. 253-264.

——. "The Work of Art in the Age of Mechanical Reproduction." *Illuminations: Essays, Aphorisms, Autobiographical Writings*. Ed. Hannah Arendt. Trans. Harry Zohn. New York: Schocken, 1969. 217-251.

Berman, Marshall. *All That Is Solid Melts Into Air: The Experience of Modernity*. 1982. Rpt. Harmondsworth, U.K.: Penguin, 1988.

Breton, André. *Nadja*. Paris: Librairie Gallimard, 1928.

Buci-Glucksmann, Christine. *Baroque Reason: The Aesthetics of Modernity*. Trans. Patrick Camiller. London: Sage, 1994.

Buck-Morss, Susan. "The *Flâneur*, The Sandwichman and the Whore: The Politics of Loitering." *New German Critique* 39 (1986): 99-140.

Cobb, Robert. "The Assassination of Paris." *New York Review of*

Books 7 (February 1980): unknown.

Cohen, Margaret. *Profane Illuminations: Walter Benjamin and the Paris of Surrealist Revolution.* Berkeley: U of California P, 1993.

Ferguson, Priscilla Parkhurst. "The Flâneur On and Off the Streets of Paris." *The Flâneur.* Ed. Keith Tester. London: Routledge, 1994. 22-42.

Foster, Hal. *The Return of the Real: The Avant-Garde at the Turn of the Century.* Cambridge, MA: MIT Press, 1996.

Higonnet, Anne, Margaret Higonnet and Patrice Higonnet. "Façades: Walter Benjamin's Paris." *Critical Inquiry* 10 (March 1984): 391-419.

Ivernel, Philippe. "Paris, Capital of the Popular Front or the Posthumous Life of the 19th Century." *New German Critique* 39 (1986): 61-84.

Koepnick, Lutz P. "Fascist Aesthetics Revisited." *Modernism/Modernity* 6.1 (January 1999): 51-74.

Paris. Guide Bleu. Paris: Hachette, 1995.

Scott, Gail. *Heroine.* Toronto: Coach House, 1987.

——. *Main Brides. Against Ochre Pediment and Aztec Sky.* Toronto: Coach House, 1993.

——. *My Paris.* Toronto: Mercury, 1999.

Shields, Rob. "Fancy Footwork: Walter Benjamin's Notes on Flanerie." *The Flâneur.* Ed. Keith Tester. London: Routledge, 1994. 61-80.

Stein, Gertrude. *How To Write.* Los Angeles: Sun & Moon, 1931.

——. *Paris France.* 1940. Rpt. New York: Liveright, 1970.

In Conversation

GAIL SCOTT, LIANNE MOYES AND COREY FROST

LM: I'm interested in new narrative and in various questions you are raising in your essays and novels, and how you are working them out in the writing – on the level of the sentence, as well as on other levels. I wanted to focus on your essays, in part because they address these questions, enacting or performing various possible responses, and in part because they have not been discussed at length in other interviews. I asked Corey to participate in order to act as a third voice, interrupting the back and forth of the interview and bringing his own thinking about new narrative to bear on the conversation. So, I'll begin by asking, are there differences for you between writing essays and writing novels?

GS: Each spills out over the edges. Spontaneously, I want to say: a big difference. There's an agenda when I write essays. Sometimes it's political and, not being a scholar, often polemical. I think I'm a good essay writer, probably because of my background in Journalism which gives me the urge to marry my passion for ideas with anecdotes. My grandfather was a superb storyteller; he used to teach us things. I sometimes prefer to put anecdotes in essays and leave them out of fiction. Yet, in both the essay and the novel –

Has she ?

though the former begins from a political or polemic or conversational impulse, and the latter from pure desire – I don't really know what the writing is about until it is written.

More and more, I wish I could write short things. Novels take the bejesus out of you. Now that the narrator is no longer omniscient, to write a novel is to confront the material of living at its most intense, to write out of a place where language, which is public, and the body, which wants to be private, spar it out. Every time I write a novel, I think, okay, this is the last. But then another big question needs to be asked. The big questions are things that can't get worked out in shorter texts, at least, not in my shorter texts. Not yet. At the same time, for better or for worse, writing a novel is profoundly about affect on some level. I think that's why it's still around. The thing that makes a novel work is that, at some point, if you succeed with your project, you touch some kind of button or nerve that is so incredible, that nobody has touched before. That's when you write a really, really good novel. You touch something. And it is about affect as a screen for all the social and political and cultural and personal and geographical particles, captured somehow in syntax, which is music. All the things that give tone to a moment in time. This surface is ever in flux. In late capitalist culture, for example, we deal majorly in romantic love; romantic love, particularly in popular culture, is the trope that ultimately signs one of the fundamental relational units of Western democracies: the family. Yet, so many domains – social and historical – come to bear on and stress and strain this word "love." Someone who lived at the time of *le Roman de la Rose*, when courtly love was in vogue, would scarcely recognize what we call love. I suppose the novel works its way along at the level of signs or tropes, such as the love trope; it's an advertising campaign declaiming the structures hidden by the billboards.

LM: If I think about your novels, and also what you're saying in "Bottom's Up," you're trying to find ways of resisting or avoiding those particular tropes of romantic love. I mean, they're there, there's a kind of –

GS: No, I want to resist what you're saying and to declare *Heroine* the only novel where I try to take on romantic love in the very structure of the novel – by deconstructing the soap opera form. But it is true that in *Main Brides*, above and beyond the *rapport de désir* between the narrator and her alleged narrative subjects – which might be a total exercise in narcissism because they might be her, all of them, or most of them, anyway, there are two portraits that involve romantic love: the lesbian coming-out romance, called "Canadian Girls," so a little distantiation just the same; and the tango piece, which is told in a distressingly drunken voice, thus a little camped up. In *My Paris*, the coda is very romantic, in a cut-up way, but it comprises only the last few pages of the novel.

LM: I meant that the novels try to do something quite different from participate in the clichés of romantic love as the major way of tapping into affect, if I'm understanding.

GS: Yes, maybe romantic love turns into something else when it crosses the gay-straight line. I don't mean better, I mean less obviously coded in a general sense. I don't REALLY think that there is anything as definitive as a line. But in *Heroine*, somehow the soap opera trope wouldn't have worked had the main relationship been gay. In romantic love between two gay people, the publicly recognizable tropes are still missing except as terrible clichés. Camp is a way of dealing with that. I think camp is one of the things I am talking about in "Bottom's Up," where there's this terrible loneliness and attempt to survive in a world where the way the subject speaks and offers herself to other people isn't necessarily understood because when people look at her, there's no sort of erotic understanding of what's going on between her and the world around her; people can't see her as she is because most of the people around her are straight. There's a section in "Bottom's Up" which talks about this woman vogueing down the street. Actually, this woman exists and she's a friend of mine; she's very beautiful and, I think, a very feminine-looking woman. But she has been known to get thrown out of women's washrooms in bars. Straight people think she's in drag; even in lesbian bars, her gender has been questioned. So it gets very, very complicated, the question of coding, of expressing the gestures of seduction.

LM: Is that one of the differences between new narrative and fiction-theory? That, in a way, fiction-theory grew out of a feminist context, and new narrative out of a queer context?

GS: Again, I want to say "yes" and, at the same time, I feel a discomfort regarding these terms, which are attempts to pin down various flights of fancy towards new identitary possibilities at a certain moment in time. I prefer the more playful and elastic French *fiction/théorie* to fiction-theory, for the emphasis in the former seems to be more on fiction than in the translated "fiction-theory." New narrative is also just an attempt to describe a turning point in fiction writing practice. So many different people in so many different ways and places – including young writers, like Corey and Anne Stone – might be identified with this experimental prose that has deep debts to both post-modern notions of writing as process and to popular culture. But the term originated in queer space. What's specific about the new narrative writing that started in San Francisco, around writers like Robert Glück, is that it emerged in the context of intense theoretical and political critical awareness about a variety of post-modern issues involving writing, the body-politic and consciousness, yet, it did not buy the "death of the subject" notion that the language poets were attached to. In Quebec, this rhymes with how *l'écriture au féminin* emerged in reaction to *le formalisme québécois.* They both spring from concerns around issues of subjectivity – new, consciously constructed and continuously disrupted subjectivities – and around generating new localisms through gossip, through performing for each other. Perhaps, in Montreal, for younger writers, the spoken word movement fulfils this function of community building.

CF: Yes, definitely. It's the community talking to itself.

I'm still not entirely satisfied with the whole conversation that happened there about affect. I got the impression, reading on the *Narrativity* website, that there was an avoidance of questions of affect or emotion. Robert Glück, for example, implies in his essay that the reaction to formalism consisted of writing with specific political meanings, as opposed to specific emotions. He doesn't talk about narrative as something that you can recuperate in order to create affect.

GS: Where you get the subject you get meaning and affect, and both queer and feminist writers resisted the death of the author on the grounds that we didn't want to get killed off before we existed. But it's not the same author; it is an author conscious of how "one" and "other" are constructed in textual practice.

LM [to GS]: In the essay "What if the writer were in bed?" the narrator tells us that the writer is in bed, "STRUGGLING between THE ACOUSTICAL,

OTHER SENSORY AFFECTS OF LANGUAGE, and – DESIRE FOR MEANING (THEORY) (IDEN-TITY?) (something to hold on to: a train schedule)" (3). I was curious, what is at stake in this relationship between the sensory and narrative, between affect and narrative?

GS: This is a tangled question. There is an intricate relationship between creating affect – which is a construction that cannot be reduced to a simple emotion – and narrating as a way of learning to know. It's a mistake to think emotion is pure, i.e. not in part a learned response, that our sensory responses are not mediated somewhat by culture. Yet, as German critic Friedrich Kittler implies when he writes, "[w]herever phones are ringing, a ghost resides in the receiver" (75), we bear essential traces of humanity, of gender, for instance, that are consistent from generation to generation. The deepest impact of a work of words happens at a point that cannot immediately be spoken. In this sense, the great novels are musical compositions. I've just been reading this incredible author Lawrence Braithwaite, an African-Canadian punk, queer writer and former Montrealer now living in Victoria, I believe. Have either of you read *Wigger*?

CF: Yeah.

GS: What'd you think of it?

CF: It's impressive, but I read it a long time ago. I found that I didn't exactly understand all the references in the subculture, so it was hard for me to access, but I thought it was very . . . well, it was thick with affect.

GS: The thing that is so incredible about his work is that when you get finished reading it, as Corey says, you're not totally sure "what's happened." He uses lots of slang, lots of argot, lots of punk talk, lots of talk of people from – in his last novel *Ratz Are Nice* – people from Jamaica, I think, their expressions, all kinds. So the narrative is very opaque in the sense that it deals in language not necessarily disseminated by the CBC. But when you get finished reading, you just feel it. Your whole body reverberates with this novel, which is ultimately not opaque at all when it comes to letting you know the ef-fects of various kinds of social oppression, marginalization and ultimately highly dignified and imaginative responses to those oppressions. As Faust says in Goethe's version, "I try to find a name for the feeling, the frenzy, and I cannot find one" (qtd. in Hejinian 19). Lyn Hejinian calls this inadequacy of speech the "lyric dilemma" (19).

The relationship between sensory affect/narrative in language is a reading/writing dialectic; it's about all of the buttons – through words and sentences, and their sound and movement – all of the buttons that can be pushed, about their tight but not exclusive, indeed, excessive, relationship to the thinking button, like the kind of deep pulsations and rhythms they can awaken in your body, the fear, the anguish, the pleasure, too. For language to have that kind of impact, it has to step out of the ordinary. You can't just use conventional narrative to do that. Braith-waite's work is exemplary in this respect, is more composition than narrative. In a world of information media, as Benjamin said brilliantly somewhere, the cause-and-effect habits, the lust for facts that the information media sets up in us, have trained us to think in a certain kind of way, to follow a certain kind of narrative. Straight narrative, which might also be called the commercial or corporate branch of story-telling, cannot solicit the kind of response that I'm looking for in writing – and reading. It just can't. The writing has to shock the mind and body. Otherwise it reproduces what is already there.

LM: This is maybe a difficult question for Gail to answer. Maybe I could ask Corey. How does Gail's writing *affect* the reader?

CF: The kind of writing I really like has an emotional structure underlying the narrative structure. *Heroine* definitely has that. In fact the way you were describing *Wigger* is similar to the way I felt reading *Heroine*. I think there is an obvious affective potential in the traditional narrative, but it is tied to the reader's relationship to the characters and what happens to them in the story. In new narrative, there's still an emotional structure but it's disconnected from the actual story; it happens underneath all the surface effects. So in *Heroine* there are all kinds of interwoven political narratives, and there are the quotidian details of the narrator's life, and so on, but it's not the break-ups and love affairs that produce the emotional effect, it's the overall pattern. The affect comes directly from the aesthetics of language in action, from the repetition of all those tiny narrative moments in the text. It's not that there's an epic story of love and revenge and politics – but there are these moments of narrative and linguistic motion. And each one has a minute emotional effect. The affect somehow grows from that. It's the same way in *My Paris*; it's a book all about details, because there's not much happening in the way of a story but you've got all of these little narrative molecules.

LM: Isn't affect working on the level of the sentence, too, insofar as the sentences are all unhinged? For example, in *My Paris*, they're quite brief.

GS: They're unhinged.

LM: Lots of things happen when they're unhinged because there are all sorts of things that we normally get through relations of syntax – like intention, subordination, relation, unity, reference – all of these things get unhinged. In "The Porous Text" you talk about movement, movement which "links within to without" (205). Questions of interiority and exteriority become unhinged, they become radically continuous, so what we normally would think of as interior, as emotion and so forth, is actually transmitted or transacted by the sentences. There's a movement back and forth because subjectivity is not discrete from the object, because the verb is open, because you're trying to create a small subject porous to the context, and so forth. So there's all this transit, passage, that gives a sense of emotion, of the so-called "interior."

GS: That's very wonderful, what you said. Maybe we need to discuss the relationship, dynamic, dialogic, dialectic, even, that gets set up between the reader and the writer, and the reading and the writing subjects.

I've been reading a book by Agamben called *The Man Without Content*. He talks about how artists, little by little, since the Middle Ages, became an object for the spectator. I think that what's changing today is that the separation of art and life, of artist and spectator, has gone so far it's come full circus. Picasso can't happen again; he seems an almost hokey balloon figure, notwithstanding the tremendous energy of his work. We're getting to a point where we look at writing or art or music or whatever, and we are no longer looking for the one great work; but rather, there is a dialectic between works, often between works in different modes of expression and those who engage with that work. Whether we're talking affect or awareness, there is new creative emphasis and space for the reader/spectator. One of my favourite writers is Carla Harryman who, in some of her texts, develops a relation of play between reader and writer; the narrative, if you can call it that, is produced at the point of engagement between the two.

It's curious in itself how the reader/writer relationship differs from circumstance to circumstance.

Heroine, for example, doesn't seem to be as interesting a book for people outside Canada as it is for people in Canada, for whom it is almost a cult object. People in Canada talk to me about it when I do readings. Elsewhere, other books of mine seem to occupy that space. Visual artists have an easier time with *My Paris*, for example, as do people in other fields, geography, and so on. At least, they respond more in the way I intended it to be read sometimes than actual, say, poets do. So it's very bizarre the way a work gets created in the middle space, the in-between, where the dots get momentarily joined. *Main Brides* is the closest thing I've ever done to a work of music; the portraits and the way the light and surface reverberate, as I see it, have a strong tonal component, but heaven knows if anyone else reads it the way I do.

CF: Yes, I think that's another way of describing how the affect comes out of the moment in the text. That's how music works, after all. It's not the story, or the song that affects you, it's the changes from note to note, key changes, and so on.

GS: That's interesting. I am currently on a campaign to get people to read prose denotatively. Like one reads poetry.

LM: Let's go from music to cinema. To the quotation by Jean-Luc Godard which opens "What if the writer were in bed?" – "Only the hand which erases everything can write" – but also to your phrase, "CINEMA OF SENTENCES." Is there a difference between the cinema of sentences and what Godard is saying? The cinema of sentences strikes me as being much more Benjaminian; it involves montage, piecing together bits of other people's words. I found an interesting tension between the gesture of cleaning the slate and the gesture of piecing together all of the bits.

CF: I think piecing together, montaging quotations, is basically a process of erasure because you're erasing the original meaning of those quotations, you're erasing the voice. Using quotations is a way of unwriting those quotations.

LM: You don't see a tension, then?

CF: No, I think these activities are really one and the same.

LM [to GS]: I saw the Godard as a very presumptuous gesture. And the Benjamin, with its emphasis on intertextuality, and so forth, as much more in keeping with your small subject. Of course, in "The Porous Text," you were talking about the contradiction the small subject faces in being small, because it has to be small enough to take in the *heteroglossia* but, at the same time, big enough to take the risk of doing that (203).

GS: Corey really has something there. Perhaps contradictorily, I also had this idea in writing *My Paris* of constructing this small subject out of the *heteroglossia*, piece by piece, to create a subject so "full of holes" she could reveal the negative aspects of the cultural baggage you pack to travel, biases, etc. Additionally, in a funny way in *My Paris*, and maybe in all of my novels, there's a huge gap in the writing subject. On her first trip to Paris, for example, she tries to be the small, material, objectified, therefore, somewhat abject, subject. But she can't really function as a person. I mean, she never gets laid, for example, so she has to come back later with a lover in order to experience that other side of her. So, yes, I think there is a kind of tension that's a huge puzzle for me in writing and thinking.

LM: I wanted to ask you more about sentences. In "Bottom's Up," the narrator wonders if she is "projecting [her own] accumulated lack on unsuspecting bodies," thereby sentencing them. So sentencing ends up being something quite binding – and, at the same time, potentially unbinding, unbounded.

GS: Binding, in the sense that the sentence ends with a period. And there's a way the sentence operates perpetually a little bit in the past, one beat behind, because you almost have to look over your shoulder to write a sentence. A sentence, even if only for a minute at a time, is a way of putting a final point, making a judgement regarding what is perceived. My sense, from talking to many poets, is that poetry is a superior form inasmuch as it does not traffic in this backward glance. Or, at least, can choose not to. It works both ways. While there is an element of judgement in sentences, at the same time, and it's the reason why I write fiction, I think of sentences as things that go back and forth between people and back and forth between groups of people. You have to take the risk of that momentary attempt to string things together, to pin things down, in order to communicate with another person. These attempts are always failed examples of our humanity but, at the same time, they are attempts.

LM: You are saying that sentences are binding. But I took from the essays that one of your projects is to open up the sentence, to unhinge or unbind the sentence. So even though you have to take the risk of that binding, that judgement, that particular movement from A to B, you're trying to find ways of complicating that movement, making it more tenuous, stalling it, making its direction less decidable.

GS: In the kind of narrative I try to write and the kinds of subjects I try to create, I try to make this statement that ends with "PERIOD" as fleeting as possible. I was trying to achieve that in *My Paris* with the present participle, that is, trying to make the sentence more porous.

LM: Has that been a project always? In your other texts?

GS: I've always been interested in sentences as a means of playing with parts and partialities, of questioning the relationships between things, between the subject and object to name the most obvious. In my desire to pack a maximum amount of suggestion of all types into sentences, I try to play with them on their sonorous register, as well. And then, there are all kinds of ways of putting sentences together, in paragraphs and on pages, that can also make a sentence less binding, if you like. Some writers today, for example – well, you do this sometimes, Corey – will write a sentence, and then they'll contradict that sentence with the next sentence. I did that in *Heroine*; the writer would make a statement and then she would criticize herself for making that statement by denying it.

In the current novel I'm writing, the first part has a fly on the wall as the narrator; (s)he's a fly on the wall in a psychological sense, for example, when you're a kid and something awful is happening to you or to your family, you might imagine yourself as a fly on the wall watching. Anyway, this fly speaks in every possible register of language, and often the language falls apart completely and falls into other languages and dialects. So you can question the sentence in all kinds of different ways. But, you know, when you say to somebody [slaps table], "that's what I think, period!" That's what a period is, you know? That's the intention of the sentence; it doesn't mean that's what the sentence really is, but the intention is to get to that period!

CF: I like what you were saying about how you can contradict one sentence with the next sentence and it changes the first one entirely. The meaning of the sentence is never really determined until it's in a context. You can have a sentence that is bounded grammatically, very complete. Yet the meaning is far from bounded because it depends entirely on what comes after it.

LM: Let's shift ground again. What did Robert Glück say about the narrator as bottom? You mention it in the notes to "Bottom's Up." Does it have to do, in part, with your thinking about the small subject?

GS: Well, if you think of the omniscient narrator as being the ultimate "top" in sexual terms, the other extreme might be a narrator as bottom. If that narrator takes control, it's in a completely different way: control through submission, and seduction in a submissive sort of way; it's by making herself or itself or himself small, pretending to be small. But then, are you really small if you're actually in power through seduction? I like to turn around all those things.

LM: You mentioned to me the last time we talked that "Bottom's Up" was a kind of manifesto, your most recent manifesto on writing. That struck a chord with me. A manifesto performs the kinds of subversive writing practices it announces. Many of the texts in *Tessera*'s issue on fiction-theory, the manifestory moment of fiction-theory, at least in English Canada, do that. "Bottom's Up" does that. And the essay is in the first issue of *Narrativity*; in other words, it is part of a collective project that you're engaged in. "Bottom's Up" is more meditative than most manifestos; it doesn't have the feel of a moment of exuberant energy being propelled or projected outward. That led me to wonder, is it the small subject's manifesto?

GS: A delicious suggestion. I suppose it can be a small subject's manifesto. I wish it were less melancholic. I don't think I have tried to discern, therein, how the moment of *Narrativity* might be distinguished from when we first started talking about *fiction/théorie?* Our discussions of *fiction/théorie* were really focused on writing but it was part of a larger political movement. Both feminist identitary issues and the queer ones have been essential to my understanding of what it means for me to write, to "relate" things. The *Narrativity* website is a grand place for explorations of ways and means of plying one's craft. The looseness of the word "queer" is helpful here. I feel very free in this space, feel that I do not have to look over my shoulder.

CF: Can I ask a question about the *Narrativity* website? I was wondering when you and the others came up with the idea – did you think of it as a kind of manifesto or way of defining what new narrative is for other people who hadn't yet heard of it, maybe?

GS: Definition of anything was the last thing on my mind – nor do I believe that was anyone's intention. I personally would like the web journal to be a site that would allow people to read experimental fiction with all its implications. Also, in the twentieth century, there came to be, particularly around modernism and its offshoots, including language poetry, such a highly developed series of discourses of poetics.

CF: Fiction became such a mainstream thing.

GS: Yes. This is the first attempt I know of to offer an ongoing site where avant-garde fiction can be displayed, examined, taken apart, and played with, rather than talking of prose writing as if it were necessarily about something.

LM: In "What if the writer were in bed?" you go back to your collection of essays *Spaces Like Stairs* and excerpt it. I'm curious, are there questions or issues that you began working on in *Spaces Like Stairs* that you're still working on in your current essays?

GS: Let's see. What can I say? The most obvious thing joining these two currents is a desire to project an unbounded subject, to write "I" in the plural or, at least, to question the singular writing subject through various devices implying various solidarities. I am obviously a writer who's interested in ethical questions, yet cannot quite fit into the radical feminist mode or any other mode implying a direct relationship between politics and writing. At the same time, my writing is more political than that of a writer who has never been involved in social or political movements. Both feminism and Marxism, revisited, i.e. somewhat bent for my own fictional purposes, have been huge to me. Feminism taught me my life was important, ergo I was, therefore, I could write. It gave me an audience, it opened a space where I could think about language. Marxism and, recently, the fascinating Benjaminian version of that kind of dialectics, has taught me about the material nature of things, including language.

I am a so-called *avant-gardist* – we've got to find a new word – in the sense that writing, for me, is about dislocating thinking. That's consistent throughout all my writing practice, from *Spaces Like Stairs* to whatever is happening with *Narrativity* right now. I see this dislocation as happening in concert and in conversation with others. Excellent writing, whatever its mode, achieves dislocation on some level. The shock of realizing one is seeing the world differently can be sudden, violent – what Benjamin called after Breton "profane illumination"(179) – or can be cumulative as in fine storytelling. I admire the work of Dany Laferrière, for instance; he's a great storyteller.

LM: I'm glad you used the word "ethical," because it reminded me that I had started to feel throughout the essays, as well as in the novels, that you were after a kind of, or asking questions about an, ethics of narration.

GS: Would I say that? An ethics of narration? I fear we're getting a little out of my element here.

LM: Or, an ethics of sentencing? An ethics of producing sentences?

GS: I immediately get an image of a judge with a pink mallet, or something. [laughter] I don't know. I like the conjunction of the word "ethics" with the word "narrativity." But ultimately, I am a storyteller. Your question seems like a question for a scholar.

LM: I'm thinking in terms of your questions in "Bottom's Up" about the narrator's relationship to others, and her relation to self. I mean, in any of her given encounters, it is her openness to, or questioning of, her response; it is her confronting what she hadn't expected or what she was going to say about a person . . . that makes me think. As a reader, I'm not allowed to fall into an expected sequence of encounters or descriptions of those encounters. I'm confronted in the same way she is. That to me is very much a question of ethics. Not ethics in a sense of right and wrong, morality, but ethics in the sense of relations vis-à-vis otherness, difference, those kinds of relations, in Irigaray's way of thinking, through Levinas, about what would be an ethical stance in relationship to another subject. I suppose I mean the challenge of being open to otherness that is radically, inconceivably different from oneself. That seemed to be a part of the small subject.

GS: It is true that I am very troubled by how "one" and "other" meet in syntax and how that might trouble, if challenged, narrative shape and narrative postures. That's why I get put in the category called unsatisfactorily "*avant-garde* writing." I almost feel that this question of ethics in the kind of fiction I write is a matter of *techné*, of honing one's craft endlessly in the process of revealing the exigencies of one's time. A key word is fluidity. Gertrude Stein said somewhere about sentences that they had a balance which was the balance of a space completely not filled but created by something moving. These sentences, this movement, is not a fluidity of self, for it is not my self that is happening in fiction. "I," for me, is plural and on the run; were it to stop, become fixed, the writing would be in the past. Look how we keep altering terms used for racialization and no matter what terms they are, they still amount to racialization. I suppose the question that underscores my thinking until now in a critical sense has been how to organize subject-fluidity in language. This was at the outset a feminist question. I have felt ever since I started writing that we're all in this together, we're all mixed up, that somehow the boundaries dissolve and need to dissolve and reconstitute endlessly. I suppose the effort to explore dynamic possibilities for boundaries between self and other is a response to living in a world which is not and never has been monolithic. My family background is not monolithic either. It is a huge puzzle for me how language gets melted down into this meeting-place between people who are really different, who maybe even hate each other. I don't know where ethical intention starts and stops. My essays try to articulate the *chantier* of what is being attempted in the fiction process, a grammar where the social and the heart meet. And there is the return of what was repressed at the beginning of the interview: that old ventriloquist, the "heart"!

WORKS CITED

Benjamin, Walter. "Surrealism." *Reflections: Essays, Aphorisms, Autobiographical Writings*. Ed. Peter Demetz. Trans. Edmund Jephcott. New York: Schocken, 1986. 177-192.

Hejinian, Lyn. "La Faustienne." *Poetics Journal* 10 (1998): 10-29.

Kittler, Friedrich. *Gramophones, Film, Typewriter*. Trans. Geoffrey Winthrop-Young and Michael Wutz. Stanford, CA: Stanford UP, 1999.

Scott, Gail. "Bottoms Up." *Narrativity* 1 (1999): n. pag. Ed. Mary Burger, Robert Glück, Camille Roy and Gail Scott. Internet. 21 May 2001. Available HTTP: www.sfsu.edu/~newlit/narrativity.html.

——. "The Porous Text, or the Ecology of the Small Subject, Take 2." *Chain*. Special Topic: Different Languages 5 (1998): 202-206. Ed. Jena Osman and Juliana Spahr. Internet. Available HTTP: www.temple.edu/chain.

——. "What if the writer were in bed? On Narrative." *Matrix* 48 (1996): 3-6.

A Brief Biography of Gail Scott

Born in Ottawa, Gail Scott's early childhood was spent in Calgary, Vancouver, Winnipeg; from the age of eight until leaving home, she lived in a bilingual community in Eastern Ontario, about 90 miles from Montréal. Her maternal grandparents were American and Métis; her paternal grandparents were blue-collar workers from England and Scotland who arrived in Winnipeg in time for the General Strike. She has a daughter (Anna Isacsson, born 1971). She lives in Montréal, between the mountain and The Main, and her writing attempts to come to grips with the language produced in her head out of the French, English, Portuguese, Greek, and other musics that comprise the soundtrack of that neighbourhood.

Scott received a B.A. in English and Modern Languages from Queen's University and she studied French literature at the graduate level at Université de Grenoble, France. As a young writer she moved to Montréal where she worked as a journalist from 1967 to 1980. One of the rare bilingual English-speaking reporters in that period, she covered key political and cultural events in Quebec for an English-Canadian audience. During this time, Scott was a founding editor of the alternative political publication *The Last Post* (1970), the feminist magazine *Des luttes et des rires des femmes* (late 1970s), and the French-language cultural magazine *Spirale* (1979-1983). Written at a time when she was leaving journalism, Scott's first book, *Spare Parts* (1981), is a collection of short stories which parody journalistic style. In these stories, non sequiturs disturb the logic of cause and effect, the extraordinary clashes with the matter-of-fact, and strings of simple sentences generate emotional charges which trouble the even surface of newspaper writing.

The 1980s were a period of tremendous growth and activity for feminist writers in Canada and Quebec. Supporting herself by teaching Journalism at Concordia University (1980-1991), Gail Scott was a central figure in both francophone and anglophone feminist circles. As a bilingual woman living in Quebec who found, and continues to find, sustenance in French-language culture, her writing bears traces of French rhythms and syntax, as well as of sustained interaction with Quebec intellectuals such as Nicole Brossard and France Théoret. *La théorie, un dimanche* (1988), a collection of texts which emerged from the discussions of a feminist writing group in which she participated, speaks of the importance of the writing subject and, more specifically, the gendered writing subject, at a time when it was widely held that the author was "dead." Throughout the 1980s, Scott was instrumental in making the formally innovative writing of French-speaking women available to English-speakers across Canada. Toward this end, she co-founded and worked as Quebec editor for the bilingual journal *Tessera* (1984-1989) and she continues to translate the writing of Quebec women such as France Théoret (*Laurence*, 1998).

The essays collected in *Spaces Like Stairs* (1989) give a sense not only of the range of issues which preoccupy the francophone and anglophone feminist communities during the 1980s, but also of the specificity of Scott's location in-between, at the meeting points of, languages and cultures. Scott has become an important figure in the field of anglophone writing in Quebec because of her engagement with the question of what it means to live and write "in translation." While some English-language writers lament the loss of a tradition of literature in English in Quebec, Gail Scott is among those who celebrate the strength of French-language culture and the possibility of a marked or "minor" practice of English. That her first two novels, *Heroine* (1987) and *Main Brides* (1993), were published by Coach House Press, a small press which specialized in formal innovation as well as in translations of writing from Quebec, is no coincidence.

Gail Scott is well-known in experimental-writing circles throughout North America. In 1985, after giving a prose workshop at the West Word Summer School Retreat, a feminist writing workshop held in Vancouver, she participated in The New Poetics Colloquium, a cross-cultural discussion between Canadian and American poets. Since the mid-1980s, along with American writers such as Carla Harryman and Robert Glück, Scott has generated a highly innovative practice of, and discourse on, narrative. As a co-editor of the web magazine *Narrativity*, launched in 1999, Scott's sense of "new narrative" brings together her interest in making sentences vehicles of music and affect, in creating a writing subject porous enough to take in the world around her yet coherent enough to act and write, in re-imagining romantic love in queer terms, and in exploring the oblique relations among language, bodies and politics.

In Scott's novels, narrative becomes a fleeting, incomplete structure available only indirectly through a glance, an encounter, a detail, a persistent figure or phrase. There is no privileged centre of consciousness. Each of the novels flirts with the auto-biographical by engaging the writer's experience, for example, of the leftist and *indépendantiste* move-ments of the 1970s, of Montréal in decline in the 1980s and 1990s, or of a six-month *séjour* in Paris in 1993 (*My Paris*, 1999). At the same time, each novel presents writer, narrator, character and reader as parts of a fictional construction, as participants in a complex play of desire, identification and projection. The translation of Scott's novels into several lan-guages along with the invitations to read and to lecture in various countries attest to her international reputation. She is one of the foremost avant-garde writers in Canada.

Bibliography

WORKS BY AND ABOUT GAIL SCOTT

BOOKS

Spare Parts. Toronto: Coach House, 1981.

Heroine. Toronto: Coach House, 1987; Talonbooks, 1999.

Héroïne [*Heroine*]. Trans. Susanne de Lotbinière-Harwood. Montreal: Les Éditions du remue-ménage, 1988.

Meine fragwürdige Heldin [*Heroine*]. Trans. Gerhard Dohler. Hamburg: Rowohlt, 1990.

La théorie, un dimanche. With Louky Bersianik, Nicole Brossard, Louise Cotnoir, Louise Dupré and France Théoret. Montreal: Les Éditions du remue-ménage, 1988.

Spaces Like Stairs: Essays. Toronto: Women's Press, 1989.

Main Brides: Against Ochre Pediment and Aztec Sky. Toronto: Coach House, 1993; Talonbooks, 1997.

Les Fiançées de la Main [*Main Brides*]. Trans. Paule Noyart. Montreal: Leméac, 1999.

Laurence: A Novel. By France Théoret. Trans. Gail Scott. Toronto: Mercury, 1998.

My Paris: A Novel. Toronto: Mercury, 1999.

The Sailor's Disquiet. By Michael Delisle. Trans. Gail Scott. Toronto: Mercury, 2000.

SHORT STORIES

"Elisabeth Rides Again." *Journal of Canadian Fiction* 30 (1980): 89-105.

"Petit Larcin." Trans. Roger Des Roches. *La Nouvelle barre du jour* 107 (Nov. 1981): 53-60.

"'Le Baiser' d'Edvard Munch, revu et corrigé." Trans. Danielle Laplante. In *La théorie, un dimanche*. 67-78.

"'The Kiss' by Edvard Munch, Revisited." *Massachusetts Review* 31 (Spring-Summer 1990): 125-131.

"There's No Such Thing as Repetition." *Books in Canada* 23.5
     (Summer 1994): cover, 8-11.

ESSAYS AND CONVERSATIONS

"SP/ELLE: Spelling Out the Reasons." A *Tessera* Editorial Discus-
     sion. With Barbara Godard, Daphne Marlatt and Kathy
     Mezei. *Room of One's Own* 8.4 (Jan. 1984): 4-18.
"Finding Her Voice." *Canadian Forum* 65 (June-July 1985):
     39-41, 44.
"Des espaces en escalier." Trans. Susanne de Lotbinière-Harwood.
     La Nouvelle barre du jour 172 (1986): 31-36.
"Virginia and Colette on the Outside Looking In." *A/Mazing
     Space: Writing Canadian Women*. Ed. Shirley Neuman and
     Smaro Kamboureli. Edmonton: Longspoon, 1986. 367-373.
"Une féministe au carnaval." In *La théorie, un dimanche*. 37-66.
"Face to Face." Interview with Linda Leith. *Matrix* 28 (Spring
     1989): 23-24.
"On the edge of change." Interview with Barbara Carey. *Books in
     Canada* 18.6 (Aug.-Sept. 1989): 15, 17-19.
"Dialogue on Quebec 1970." With Karen Gould, Mary Jean
     Green, Robert Schwartzwald, Jean-Marc Piotte, Pauline
     Julien. *Quebec Studies* 11 (Fall 1990-Winter 1991): 63-73.
"'A Very Rhythmic and Almost Conversational Surface.'" Inter-
     view with Janice Williamson. *Sounding Differences: Conver-
     sations with Seventeen Canadian Women Writers*. Ed. Wil-
     liamson. Toronto: U of Toronto P, 1993. 249-265.
"Theorizing Fiction Theory." With Barbara Godard, Daphne
     Marlatt and Kathy Mezei. Ed. Godard. *Collaboration in the
     Feminine: Writings on Women and Culture from Tessera*.
     Toronto: Second Story, 1994. 53-62.
"In Conversation." With Barbara Godard, Susan Knutson,
     Daphne Marlatt and Kathy Mezei. In *Collaboration* 120-126.
"What We Talk About on Sundays." With Nicole Brossard, Louky
     Bersianik, Louise Cotnoir, Louise Dupré, France Théoret and
     Barbara Godard. In *Collaboration* 127-135.
"Vers-ions Con-verse: A Sequence of Translations." With Barbara
     Godard, Susan Knutson, Daphne Marlatt, Kathy Mezei and
     Lola Lemire Tostevin. In *Collaboration* 153-161.

"Feminist Mothers, Feminist Daughters." Part One. *Canadian Dimension* 28.1 (Jan.-Feb. 1994): 37-39.

"Feminist Mothers, Feminist Daughters." Part Two. *Canadian Dimension* 28.2 (Mar.-Apr. 1994): 37-38.

"What if the writer were in bed? On Narrative." *Matrix* 48 (1996): 3-6.

"Elixir for Thinking: Carla Harryman's *There never was a rose without a thorn.*" *West Coast Line* 31.2 (Fall 1997): 144-148.

"My Montréal: Notes of an Anglo-Québécois Writer." *Brick* 59 (Spring 1998): 4-9.

"Oral Tapestry: Gail Scott." Interview with Beverly Daurio. *The Power to Bend Spoons: Interviews with Canadian Novelists.* Ed. Daurio. Toronto: Mercury, 1998. 160-167.

"The Porous Text, or the Ecology of the Small Subject, Take 2." Special Topic: Different Languages. *Chain* 5 (1998): 202-206. Ed. Jena Osman and Juliana Spahr. Online. Internet. Available HTTP: www.temple.edu/chain.

"Miroirs inconstants." In dossier "Écrire en anglais au Québec: un devenir minoritaire?" Ed. Lianne Moyes. *Quebec Studies* 26 (Fall 1998-Winter 1999): 23-25.

"Bottoms Up." *Narrativity* 1 (1999): n. pag. Ed. Gail Scott, Mary Burger, Robert Glück and Camille Roy. Online. Internet. Available HTTP:www.sfsu.edu/~newlit/narrativity/home.html.

"Cusps: An Interview with Gail Scott." By Corey Frost. *Matrix* 54 (Aug. 1999): 58-67. Rpt. as "Some Other Kind of Subject, Less Bounded." *How2* 1.4 (Sept. 2000): n. pag. Online. Available HTTP:www.scc.rutgers.edu/however/v1_4_2000/current/workbook/inde x.html#interview.

PUBLICATIONS ABOUT THE WORK
OF GAIL SCOTT

Blumberg, Marcia. "Reading Gail Scott's *Heroine*: A Triple Lens of Sighting/Citing/Siting." *Open Letter* 8.2 (Winter 1992): 57-69.

Chisholm, Dianne. "The City of Collective Memory." *GLQ: A Journal of Gay and Lesbian Studies* 7.2 (2001): 195-243.

Davey, Frank. "Totally Avant-garde Woman: *Heroine.*" *Post-National Arguments: The Politics of the Anglophone-Canadian*

Novel since 1967. Toronto: U of Toronto P, 1993. 210-222.

Freiwald, Bina Toledo. "'Towards the Uncanny Edge of Language': Gail Scott's Liminal Trajectories." *Essays on Canadian Writing* 54 (Winter 1994): 60-79.

Godard, Barbara. "*Heroine* by Gail Scott." *Borderlines* 11 (Spring-Summer 1988): 50-51.

——. "Writing from the Border." *Trois* 11.1-2 (1996): 169-180.

Henderson, Jennifer. "Femme(s) Focale(s): *Main Brides* and the Post-Identity Novel." *Studies in Canadian Literature* 20.1 (1995): 93-114.

Hill, Gerald. "Across References: A *Heroine* Dictionary." *West Coast Line* 25.2 (Fall 1991): 45-56.

Irvine, Lorna. "Words on the Prowl: Quebec Literature and Gail Scott's *Heroine*." *Quebec Studies* 9 (1989-90): 111-120.

Kadar, Marlene. "Whose Life Is It Anyway? Out of the Bathtub and into the Narrative." *Essays on Life Writing: From Genre to Critical Practice*. Toronto: U of Toronto P, 1992. 152-161.

Kelly, Peggy. "Fiction Theory as Feminist Practice in Marlatt's *Ana Historic* and Scott's *Heroine*." *Open Letter* 9.4 (Fall 1995): 69-98.

Leahy, David. "*Running in the Family*, *Volkswagen Blues* and *Heroine*: Three Post/Colonial Post-Modernist Quests?" *Kunapipi* (Aarhus, Denmark) 14.3 (1992): 67-82.

Majzels, Robert. "Crosscurrents in the Main Stream: The Politics of the Subject in Gail Scott's *Main Brides*." *Matrix* 44 (Fall 1994): 14-18.

Markotic, Nicole. "Freedom's Just Another Word/for Nothin' Left to Close/Desire Constructing Desire Constructing in Gail Scott's *Heroine*." *Tessera* 16 (Summer 1994): 84-96.

Norton, Camille. "After Reading Gail Scott's *Spaces Like Stairs*." *Trivia: A Journal of Ideas* 15 (Fall 1989): 70-80.

Rocard, Marcienne. "*Heroine* de Gail Scott: La Romancière narcissique et son double." *Annales du centre de recherches sur l'amérique anglophone* 21 (1996): 85-92, 197.

Servinis, Ellen. "Urban Space and Barstool Flanerie in Gail Scott's *Main Brides*." Special Topic: Writing Canadian Space/Ecrire l'espace canadien. *Studies in Canadian Literature* 23.1 (1998): 250-263.

Webb, Margaret. "Long Time Coming: Gender Performances in Gail Scott's *Heroine* and *Main Brides*." *West Coast Line* 29.1 (Spring-Summer 1995): 78-88.

List of Contributors

Dianne Chisholm researches and teaches modernism and modernity, with emphasis on women's modernism. Her book-in-progress, *Queer Constellations: Fictions of Space in the Wake of the City*, uses Walter Benjamin's critical models to analyze representations of social-sexual space in experimental narratives of late-twentieth-century inner-city lesbian and gay life.

Poet, theorist, editor, and critic, Frank Davey is Carl F. Klinck Professor of Canadian Literature at the University of Western Ontario. He was the Coach House Press editor of *Heroine* on its publication in 1987. His long prose meditation *Living and Dying* will be published by ECW Press in the spring of 2002.

Corey Frost is a writer and text-based performance artist interested in narrative from a creative and critical point of view. His M.A. thesis at Université de Montréal was a work of fiction/theory about writing his novel, *headless*. He has published several chapbooks and his work has appeared in *Matrix* and *Rampike*, in the web-journal *Narrativity*, and on his own CD-ROM, *Bits World: Exciting Version*.

Barbara Godard teaches at York University where she writes on Canadian and Quebec cultures and on feminist and literary theory. Her recent publications include "Notes from the Cultural Field: Canadian Literature from Identity to Hybridity" (ECW, 2000) and "Une Littérature en devenir: Le Dynamisme de l'institution littéraire et la réception des écrivaines québécoises au Canada anglais" (*Voix et images*, 1999), winner of the Vinay-Darbelnet Prize (2000). She is editor of *Collaboration in the Feminine: Essays on Women and Culture from* Tessera (1994) and of *Intersexions: Issues of Race and Gender in Canadian Women's Writing* (1996; Women's Press, 2001). Currently she is translating Nicole Brossard's *Journal Intime* and editing *Translation Studies in Canada: Institutions, Practices, Discourses, Texts*.

Carla Harryman's most recent books include an experimental novel, *The Words: After Carl Sandburg's Rootabaga Stories and Jean-Paul Sartre* (O Books, 1999) and a collection of prose and prose poetry writings, *There Never Was a Rose without a Thorn* (City Lights, 1995). *Gardener of Stars*, a novel, is forthcoming from Atelos Press. Her most recent play, *Performing Objects Stationed in Platform on the Sub(Urban) World*, was written at the invitation of the Poetry Centre at Oxford Brooks University and received its first staged reading there in April 2001. In 1995, Harryman moved from the San Francisco Bay Area to the Metro Detroit Area where she teaches Creative Writing, Women's Studies, and Literature at Wayne State University and co-organizes Black Mouth Readers Theater in the Cass Corridor neighbourhood of Detroit. She is currently working on a collection of essays on the writings of Kathy Acker.

Jennifer Henderson is a postdoctoral fellow in the Department of English at the University of Toronto and an editor of *Tessera*. She has published articles on Canadian literature and criticism, film, and recovery discourse. *Conducting Selves* is a book forthcoming from the University of Toronto Press.

Nicole Markotic teaches English Literature and Creative Writing at the University of Calgary, is Poetry Editor for Red Deer Press, and is one of the editors on the feminist collective of *Tessera* magazine. Her most recent book is a collection of poetry, *Minotaurs & Other Alphabets* (Wolsak & Wynn). She is currently working on a critical book regarding the constructions and representations of the problem body.

Lianne Moyes teaches in the Département d'études anglaises at Université de Montréal. She works on various forms of cross-border writing including fiction theory, bilingual writing, franco-Ontarian and anglo-Quebec writing. She also works on intertextuality and feminist literary history, and on contemporary feminist appropriations of the baroque. She is co-editor of *Adjacencies: Minority Writing in Canada*, forthcoming from Guernica and, since 1993, has been co-editor of the feminist periodical *Tessera*.

Camille Norton is a poet and essayist. She is Associate Professor of English at the University of the Pacific Stockton and co-editor of *Resurgent: New Writing by Women* (University of Illinois Press, 1992). Her work has been published in *Field: Contemporary Poetry and Poetics* and in *How2*, an on-line journal of women and experimental writing.

Sherry Simon teaches in the Département d'études françaises at Concordia University. She is the author of *Le Trafic des langues* (Boréal, 1994), *Gender in Translation* (Routledge, 1996) and *Hybridité culturelle* (Ile de la tortue, 1999), and has most recently co-edited, with Paul St-Pierre, *Changing the Terms: Translating in the Postcolonial Era* (University of Ottawa Press, 2000).